Contents

D1798002

Dedication
Acknowledgements
Author's note

Dedication

For my husband: after the pain, peace.

Acknowledgements

To offer effective comfort alongside practical support, in the immediate aftermath of suicide, requires immense self-control and strength of character. My mother possesses both these qualities in abundance: by her resolute spirit and determined practicality, she set the standards which I sought to uphold while working my way through the trauma of my husband's unnatural death. Those same qualities of character are evident in my two sons, who have borne the agonising fact of their father's suicide with unflinching courage, and offered me every encouragement as this book gradually took shape. I'm proud to belong to such a family, to whom I owe so much.

In addition, the emotional roller-coaster of recovery has been made infinitely more bearable by the unfailing support of my wider family and friends. My family and lifelong friends have provided the profound comfort arising from a shared past and a thorough knowledge of character, while the friends I've made since my husband's death have proved to be additional points of light, all helping the darkness of horror to recede.

I'm also greatly indebted to my professional team, particularly my solicitor and my proof reader, each of whom rapidly became a trusted confidante. Also to my friends with experience of the publishing and media worlds, whose willingness to offer advice, and to share their knowledge, has been invaluable.

My heartfelt thanks to all concerned.

Author's note

Names have been changed as necessary, both to protect the privacy of those most closely involved, and also to shield others who were inadvertently caught up in the tragedy which occurred in their midst.

3

Chapter 1: Beyond recall

"As I've already told you, my husband is deceased."

"But he's the principal account holder, so for security reasons I may only speak to him."

At this point in the conversation, it occurred to me that holding a séance might save a lot of soul-searching, and would definitely save a lot of time, especially if it could be conducted by phone as a sort of celestial conference call. This didn't appear to be an option on the telephone adviser's computer screen, though, which was a great pity as it would have enabled me to kill several birds with one phone, ethereally speaking. After all, that particular adviser was by no means the only person who wanted to speak to the deceased in the wake of his suicide.

There were also, for instance, my husband's employers, who sent him a nice, chatty letter, informing him that following his 'departure' he now owed them some money, and would he please phone them? He needed to get in touch immediately because, according to their records, he was still using his work-based internet connection. All of which came as something of a surprise to me, since by that stage my husband had been dead for nearly three months.

Then, of course, there was myself as his widow, not to mention our two sons. We were all rather keen to speak to him, too.

Inevitably, there would have been some considerable delay after selecting the appropriate extension number from all the available options, as the correct adviser in this case would naturally be in a highly exalted position: Chairman of the (Ouija) Board, no less. Still, while waiting to be connected I could have chosen from a variety of suitable music, designed to encompass the full range of tastes. A loose affiliation of styles technically known as 'soul music', nowadays this should not be regarded as one single, exclusive genre, but as a totally inclusive concept, embracing everything from Robbie Williams' soothing *Angels* to the resounding *Day of Anger* from Verdi's Requiem.

In fact, the torrent of questions came from every direction – personal, corporate, official and judicial – during the early days after my husband died, but could be summed up by my own, single cry of anguish: *why?* Obviously the horror of suicide is very real indeed, although the often bizarre situations which arose from it did provide the welcome relief of humour. That, in turn, helped me to weather the emotional storm of the aftermath, and the process of my learning to deal with its practical and psychological effects.

The majority of the ever-increasing number of suicides in the UK consists of middle-aged men – like my husband. He was only four years from retirement after a successful career, with a happy marriage, robust physical health and a stable family life. In contrast to the bureaucratic idiocy of various corporate bodies, the reactions of my friends and neighbours were characterised by the most intense distress both for myself and for my sons. The shocked and incredulous response of one lifelong friend, on receiving the news of my husband's suicide, was typical:

"But you and Tom have been forever. You were supposed to go on being forever: we all thought so."

Lucy and Tom: forever. I'd thought so, too, from the time of our wedding when I was just twenty-one years old, until Tom's death more than thirty years later. But faced with the merciless legacy of suicide, the normal process of grieving for a life ended is totally eclipsed, for a time at least, by the agonising cruelty of the ending itself. The element of choice in that ending compounds the shock to a suddenly grief-stunned widow, especially when she is herself the discoverer of her husband's body. For my sons and myself, the events of that darkest day didn't only bring the present to a shuddering halt and alter the future unrecognisably, they also reached back into the past, in the inevitable search for the slightest clue to their origin.

No specific circumstance was ever identified, which could conceivably have led my husband to take his own life. There had been no discernible warning signs: suicides are capable of going to great lengths to conceal both their decision and their plans for carrying it out. So the cause appeared at first to be an impenetrable blank; some sort of catastrophic meltdown, locked away inside a collapsed mind and a disintegrated personality.

But any attempt to apply a rational perspective to this ultimately irrational act cannot prevent the instinctively emotional reaction, continually bringing me back to the longing to ask *why?* That seemingly straightforward question tormented me relentlessly, during the early stages of my sudden and grotesque widowhood. But since the dead do not reveal their secrets (even with the best efforts of modern telecommunications), I gradually learned to accept that there would be no single, decisive answer to bring a longed-for degree of comfort, however anguished the question. A complexity of factors can be glimpsed, fleetingly, as a succession of circumstances influencing a particular combination of characteristics, although these glimpses can be caught only in hindsight, which must surely be the most heartbreaking of all forms of knowledge.

Despite all the practical and emotional considerations, the sheer horror of such a death can never be totally obliterated. During the first few months I had to learn how to live alongside the enormity of that horror, in addition to the pain of loss and the inevitable feelings of guilt: *why* could I not have saved him; surely, as his wife, I should have seen this coming? Perhaps this is the main reason why suicide undoubtedly remains society's final taboo, since the search for a cause will inevitably mean exposing to view complex and intensely private relationships. When a human mind has become so damaged and distorted that death seems preferable to life, those relationships are bound to be placed under the full and glaring spotlight of official investigation, as I would come to learn through my own, intensely bitter experience.

To commit suicide is no longer regarded as a crime in the legal sense, of course. Indeed, society's attempts to remove the ugliness of association with the concept of crime have recently included the introduction of new terminology. Rather than my husband having 'committed' suicide, he can now be described, perhaps rather more gently, as having 'completed' suicide.

Unfortunately, though, there is nothing gentle about suicide. Re-labelling the act itself may have succeeded in removing the criminal association, but it cannot remove the ugliness. In stark contrast to the re-vamping of the English term, the literal translation from German is *to commit self-murder*. That seems an apt description of an act which, by its very nature, constitutes a 'crime' against the natural rhythm of life itself, and against those it leaves behind, who must deal with blighted lives in addition to broken hearts.

But as I gradually learned to accept the irrefutably ugly fact of my husband's suicide, and as I worked my way through the painful and highly eventful process of recovery, I became determined not to allow this blight to infect either the future, which remains emphatically worth living for, or the past, which deserves to be left undisturbed. Because, throughout the thirty-five years during which I knew Tom, there was no indication of our being anything other than a perfectly normal couple. The question of when suicidal thoughts first crept into his mind is one which only Tom himself could answer, as is the question of when the fatal catalyst, whatever it was, took its relentlessly final possession of him. Until then, we were an ordinary family living ordinary lives, which were suddenly engulfed by extraordinary events with no warning whatsoever. The aftermath of those events left me to deal with an agony of deeply traumatic emotions, which needed to be sloughed away, layer by painful layer, until I could finally emerge, undeniably changed but whole again. Only then could I begin to look beyond the horror, and remember a marriage which was, in fact, happy.

Although we were so young when we met – I was seventeen, Tom was twenty-one – our relationship felt absolutely right, from the very beginning. We met at the local motorbike club, which I'd joined after saving the pay from my Saturday job to buy a moped, to keep me going, literally, until I could afford to learn to drive a car. Motorbikes were Tom's lifelong passion, so at that local club, where he was known and respected and where he felt confident, he could overcome his very real shyness to become relaxed and easy to talk to. His diffidence in other situations only seemed to add to the charm of this modest, quiet but thoughtful and determined young man.

I was in the sixth form at a girls' school, enjoying life with a small circle of close friends. Tom was completely different from my contemporaries at the boys' school nearby. He seemed far more mature and was already working, while taking day-release and evening classes in technology, plus English which he needed to pass for his eventual qualifications at college. Tom was doggedly determined to establish a successful career path; to 'better himself', as his parents regularly expressed their hopes for him. With scant education and unskilled jobs themselves, Ernie and Pamela Roberts were adamant that their son should achieve far more than they themselves had done. This aspirational attitude suited Tom's character very well, with his innate capacity for unremitting hard work and his drive to succeed.

We encouraged each other as we studied, developing a deep and lasting empathy in doing so. One example stands out, even now: never a keen reader, Tom had been told to read and then discuss a major nineteenth-century classic novel of his choice, as part of his English course. He was understandably aghast at the whole prospect, and asked me if I could think of a book which might be suitable, and which he might feel comfortable to discuss. Tentatively, I suggested R L Stevenson's *Treasure Island*, mainly for its buccaneering adventure and larger-than-life characters. But I also had a more personal incentive which I hoped might appeal to Tom: he and Jim Hawkins, the endearingly modest narrator of that treasure-hunting action, shared a family surname.

Tom's maternal grandfather, Jack Hawkins, had been a successful builder, and was unfailingly encouraging of all his grandson's efforts and plans. Tom looked up to his grandfather and valued his advice, sometimes even in preference to that of his pessimistic, world-weary father. For whatever reason, though, my suggestion helped, and Tom passed his English exam. Reading for pleasure was a completely new concept for him, and although he never developed any real love of books, he would in later years occasionally read for pleasure rather than simply for work.

Tom and I were married shortly after the end of my own final exams, four years after we'd first met, and we settled easily into married life while each pursuing our own career. I was working in London, while Tom moved into the still new but already burgeoning world of information technology. He had found his niche, and his career now took off in earnest. Within a few years, he had amassed an enviable amount of technical knowledge and was taking on increasing levels of responsibility. He appeared to be thriving on his hard work and consequent success.

After the birth of our sons, Mark and Paul, we bought a family-sized house in Fleet, Hampshire. Tom needed easy access to London, and in addition to being convenient, the town was a perfect place to bring up our family. Ironically in our case, Fleet has more recently been consistently named in surveys, as being the happiest and healthiest place to live in the entire country.

It certainly suited us: Tom commuted, I taught part-time locally, and for a growing family the educational and recreational facilities were outstanding. I launched myself into local activities with a will; as the mother of two growing children it was easy, and even essential. By now Tom was working long hours, and occasionally travelling abroad on business (which he hated), so he didn't have the chance to become quite as integrated locally, but that suited him perfectly well. He was an excellent father who loved spending time with his family, while his own hobbies remained his motorbike and his garden. All of this provided a healthy antidote, I felt, to the mounting stresses at work and the increasing amounts of time spent on his computer, which now accounted for almost every evening in addition to the working day.

As Tom's expertise and level of responsibility grew, so too did the pressure of his workload. For someone as conscientious, hyper-active and introverted as Tom, this led to an increasing tendency to overwork and also to worry. Ultimately this combination of characteristics and circumstances would prove to be a dangerous one; already a perfectionist, he gradually became indisputably a workaholic.

Meanwhile, though, our sons thrived, and followed the usual path of school and university. By the time they had both left home, two years before Tom died, it was clear that they were each living happy and fully independent adult lives, which were unlikely to bring them back to Fleet, other than to see us. Tom had already started making longer-term plans, and we both felt that now was the time for a house move, before his actual retirement and our consequent reduction in income. We felt drawn to a largely unspoilt corner of the countryside where we had spent a lot of time in the pre-Fleet days, which was easily accessible and which we both loved.

We knew one unspoilt valley only slightly, having once stopped the motorbike there to enjoy a picnic beside its small, gently flowing river; now we arrived again, to view the house which was eventually to become ours. We fell in love not just with the house itself, but equally with its surroundings. A house and garden which seemed exactly right for us; a traditional village location only a short distance from a major road network; easy access to open walking country to explore and enjoy with Misty, our West Highland terrier. We looked at each other, and knew that we both felt the same: this would be an ideal place for us to enjoy our retirement together.

Chapter 2: Living in stability

Our new home was everything we'd hoped for. In the midst of the unpacking, we stood on the terrace and surveyed the lawn sloping gently down towards the riverbank. The riverbank! That in itself had always been an ideal of ours: to live beside a gently-flowing river just like this one, the fields beyond its further bank rising gradually to a belt of woodland on the horizon.

The wildly overgrown garden possessed, in estate agent's terms, 'great potential'. It also possessed a secluded hardstanding area – the perfect site for Tom's intended motorbike, where there would be plenty of room to work, conveniently concealed from the house. As happy as I would be to see Tom taking up his favourite hobby once more (particularly with his retirement approaching), I had no particular desire to look out onto a view comprising the oily innards of a partially-restored motorbike.

And then there was the house itself, 'Riverside', standing in the middle of its garden with an air of tranquillity; nothing remarkable really but, to us, representing the culmination of cherished ambitions. Mark and Paul were already planning to visit together, along with their respective girlfriends, for our first family Christmas in the country. For now, though, it was enough to know that it was ours: we had arrived.

After dark on that first evening – we had moved on a balmy September day – I persuaded Tom to take time off and walk down to the riverbank with me again. The moon was full, and tiny shards of moonlight were dancing downstream to the accompaniment of the water's gentle splashing; there seemed to be nothing else under that vast dome of night sky except the river, the fields and us. And in that brief, enchanted moment, our prospects for the future looked equally vast.

It was one of those exceptional years when summer, having decided to come late, arrives in a blaze of glory as if keen to make up for lost time, and the balmy weather continued as we began to explore further afield. Misty was clearly as delighted with her new home as we were, and just as eager to investigate her surroundings.

So too was Jerry, our much-loved tortoise, who had been part of the family for several years and, along with Misty, completed our pre-retirement household:

A couple when moving from Fleet,
Bought a house on a village main street.
"With our dog and our tort,
This is great!" was their thought;
"Hope we'll land on our paws, claws and feet."

As it seemed, indeed, we had.

Finding himself in pastures new, Jerry now set off on explorations of his own. Tom had already been hard at work with wood, hammer and nails, fencing a section of the garden to form Jerry's very own pasture and prevent him making his way down towards the riverbank, getting under the wire fence and toppling into the water. Jerry's new summer quarters were complemented by a brick-built and slate-roofed summerhouse, quickly knocked up on the cement-free, dry-wall principle, and known as the Shell Garage. We'd assumed that the new enclosure would be sufficient to contain a small tortoise: we were wrong.

Though almost blind due to cataracts, Jerry took stock of his surroundings by standing vertically on his hind legs, leaning against his new stockade on tip-claws to peer enquiringly over the top. His neck craning and his head moving slowly from side to side, Jerry looked like a highly professional reptilian land surveyor.

Having presumably got his bearings, Jerry first tried scaling the fence, but he soon realised the futility of this method, since at each attempt he would topple over and land on his back, requiring human assistance to right himself again. But being a brainy sort of tortoise (he had, after all, once attended a psychology lecture, by express invitation of the university's Vice-Chancellor), Jerry set about devising a more effective method. While we humans, believing Jerry to be safe, were busy with our own pastures new, he was busy digging his way out of his, concealing his work-in-progress under a convenient shrub.

We arrived home after Misty's evening walk to find the Shell Garage empty; not too concerned, we decided to do a quick check of Jerry's enclosure just to make sure he was there, tucked away somewhere. He wasn't. We set about searching the wider garden, only giving up when it was too dark to see. First light saw us out again, thoroughly and systematically raking (gently) through the undergrowth. Our immediate neighbours being away, we next climbed over the fence into their garden, looking like a pair of particularly inexpert burglars in gardening gloves, armed with grass rakes. We moved along to the next garden, this time knocking at the front door first to introduce ourselves and explain our quest, but still we found no sign of Jerry. So we worked our way back to our own garden, where we found Jerry just emerging nonchalantly into a patch of morning sun, from the shrubs near the fenced-off riverbank. He'd given us a very nasty moment, particularly in literal view of the river, but it had been a novel way to introduce ourselves to some more of the neighbours.

Gradually getting to know more people in the village, we began to realise how closely individuals and whole families were linked to each other. Our heads were soon reeling not only with actual names, but also with their 'connections', too, until we felt as though we'd stepped into a twenty-first century version of a Jane Austen novel. But we found only appropriate village Pride, and Prejudice against incomers non-existent, as our new neighbours gave us the kindest welcome.

That summer had been exceptionally dry, and by early autumn southeast England was officially declared to be drier than Tunisia. But it turned out to be a very wet drought we were having in our bucolic little corner of the country, as the eventual onset of autumn brought a flood to the valley, transforming our view from a gentle landscape of fields and hedgerows into a full-scale lake attracting large quantities of birds and ducks. The floodplain's transition from grassland to wetland, though short-lived, was both dramatic and beautiful, particularly when the weather cleared and tiny rippling waves formed on the vivid blue surface of the lake.

Our sloping garden was in no danger of being flooded, so we could relax and enjoy the changed view to the full, along with the extraordinary quality of light which any expanse of water tends to bring. Any expanse of water also tends to bring boats, naturally enough, but it still struck us as a picturesque novelty when we saw several canoeists paddling across the fields, in apparent formation. Although we never did launch our own very old rowing boat, we'd been enchanted by our first flood, to the extent that I began to consider changing the name of our house: from Riverside to Lakeside.

Meanwhile, we had begun making a few modest alterations to the house, one memorable occasion being the installation of an electrically-operated awning over our French windows. The workmen arrived early, got started and worked steadily, while the forecast bad weather also arrived early, got started and worsened steadily, the wind picking up all the time. Unfortunately as it turned out, regulations required the workmen to give us a demonstration of the latest compulsory safety feature: a wind sensor. By now, though, the weather was working up to a full-blown storm, so that the demonstration descended rapidly into farce. The automatic sensor sensed away madly, causing the blind to roll in and out seemingly at random, while the workmen struggled to adjust the sensor and so control the now apparently unstoppable roller mechanism. A case of the blind leading the blind, really. Luckily we'd declined the optional rain sensor, or I firmly believe we'd have been there for the rest of that storm-wracked day, standing outside the French windows being alternately drenched and caught in the crosswinds.

The flood, the awning and other similarly trivial incidents remain stored away in my memory, like old and creased photographs: treasured proof of the experiences and the laughter which Tom and I shared, when our future at Riverside looked happily assured.

We settled apparently easily into village life, whilst also pursuing our own essential activities. Although Tom was able to spend increasing amounts of time working from home, he still sometimes needed to go to the office, when he would arrange the necessary meetings over two or three consecutive days, and book a room at a nearby guest house. This arrangement appeared to be perfectly satisfactory: Tom came to know the guest house owners and seemed very relaxed there, while the proprietor took pleasure in cooking him a much-appreciated full breakfast.

Tom had never enjoyed evenings spent in a pub with colleagues, which he regarded as a waste of valuable time, so he would return to his room at the guest house as soon as he could. That meant yet more work on his laptop, of course, given Tom's conscientiousness, but he would have carried on working in his room anyway, even if he had already stayed out late with colleagues. At least this way, his personal work ethic would allow him to put his laptop aside in time to settle for a reasonable night's sleep. And so his new working routine appeared to suit him very well; in fact, he seemed to be more relaxed than he'd been for some time.

Although he was perfectly happy to see me joining in with various village activities, Tom himself clearly preferred to remain aloof. So, while I joined the village choir, ran a charity bookstall, wrote about local issues and helped to make the heraldic banners for the following summer's mediaeval-themed party, Tom preferred to dig his future vegetable patch and carry on with the interminable evenings spent on his computer.

Tom had two laptops in his study: his 'office' computer and his 'home' one, about which he was always intensely private. This 'home' version contained our household accounts and other personal matters, along with such items as the website of the motorbike club which Tom had been helping to run for some years, and the financial affairs of his bedridden aunt. I only learned after Tom's death that for some unfathomable reason, he had also been handling the financial affairs of another, perfectly able, family member.

Were there other, more insidious items which caused Tom somehow to dispose of his laptops just before he committed suicide? That deeply disturbing thought was another of the questions which tormented me after his death. But I resolutely told myself that if anything unsavoury had been going on (which would have been in absolute contrast to Tom's character, as I knew it over thirty-five years), it would have been unearthed during the exhaustive police, legal and financial investigations. And so I held to the belief that the disappearance of his computers was simply another symptom of Tom's total mental collapse, on a par with the missing funds which he 'spirited away' from our accounts online, just hours before he died.

But Tom did appear to be spending increasing amounts of time dealing with his various online matters, in addition to his continuing tendency to overwork. All of this would have been alarming, were it not for Tom's lifelong love of helping people, coupled with his relentless perfectionism. Chillingly, though, unnoticed behind the façade of Tom's apparently stable life, some form of instability must already have been developing.

The time came for the midsummer mediaeval extravaganza, and Tom was characteristically unenthusiastic at the idea of fancy dress. He chose the simplest outfit available: a belted jerkin over a leather-laced shirt, with baggy trousers tucked into boots – his own motorbike boots, naturally. I delighted in wearing a mediaeval lady's flowing gown, complete with a homemade conical hat supporting an equally flowing veil. I even abandoned my lifelong spectacles for the occasion, which worried me slightly (and probably worried Tom, too), as I am very short-sighted. Happily, though, I managed not to trip over the hog roast, or crash into any passing knights in armour, ladies, jesters, or even the King himself.

The mediaeval feast was generally hailed as a great success. Looking again at the photos of that carefree summer's revelry, I see Tom smiling into the camera. Perhaps it is only my imagination, in the light of subsequent events, causing me to see a hint in his eyes that he is not entirely comfortable...

Once again, summer turned gradually to autumn, and then we began to look forward to our second Christmas at Riverside. How lucky we are, I thought happily, to have made the move from suburbia to a village, and to a home so perfect for us. The past was secure, with our sons grown up and successfully established in their adult lives; the present seemed as good as anyone could wish for; the future looked promisingly rosy.

But the rural idyll of our life in a traditional village was about to be hideously shattered.

Chapter 3: A waking nightmare

It started as a perfectly ordinary Saturday morning; that quiet, unassuming weekend between Christmas and New Year when nothing ever happens.

Our neighbour, Angela, had been widowed a week previously, and Tom and I had been doing all we could to help her, including walking her dog along with our own. That morning, we found Angela struggling with the lock on her back door, which had just broken. Tom looked at it, decided what needed to be done, and told Angela he would come round with the necessary tools, probably sometime that afternoon. As ever, he was genuinely pleased at the prospect of helping someone, and was in apparently good spirits as we set off from Angela's house. We walked the two dogs across the fields behind the village, in cold, bright winter sunshine. As always, we gazed with affectionate pride at the rear view of our house, with its expanse of garden still looking like a rather blank but excitingly fresh canvas. As we strolled, we discussed plans for the forthcoming re-fit of our bathroom, which had been booked to start shortly after our imminent New Year trip to visit Mark, now living hundreds of miles away. Our local village builder/plumber was glad of a major job like this at a usually slack time of the year, and we were due to meet with him in the next couple of days to finalise one or two outstanding details. Tom was rather tense about the whole project, as it would be the first time he had ever employed someone else to undertake even as large a job as this one. Previously, he had always completed all building, electrical and plumbing work himself, and taken great pride in doing so. Now, though, he had finally acknowledged that he no longer had the time. He would undoubtedly have felt that keenly.

The dog walk finished, and Angela's dog duly returned to her, the day proceeded on its usual course. Tom drove my mother and me to the next village, for coffee at our favourite café; he was always particularly happy to sit at the table by the window, and look out at the café's small but well-stocked garden. Back at home and apparently content, Tom pottered in our own garden and then, over a light lunch, I asked him whether he had any plans for the afternoon, while I would be taking my mother home after the Christmas holiday. It had been a truly happy and relaxed Christmas; Paul had left to return to work in the West Country the previous day, cheerfully waved off by the rest of us. Tom's reply to my enquiry, in perfectly even-sounding tones, was:

"I'm going to have a rest this afternoon."

Perhaps I was slightly surprised by his choice of phrase, as he had never been a 'resting' sort of person; at any rate it was certainly not a phrase I had ever heard him use before. But he had shifted another large load of compost that morning, ready for use, so I automatically assumed he intended to spend the afternoon digging it into his future vegetable patch. Or perhaps he simply meant that, on reflection, he would prefer to do that rather than going to Angela's house to mend the lock on her back door, as he had suggested to her that morning. After all, Tom had never been the type to sit down and read a book, or watch television; his way of relaxing had always been by working out his seemingly endless stock of energy physically, in the house or garden, or on a car or motorbike. So I saw nothing ominous in a phrase which was, with the cold and bleak illumination of hindsight, rather out of character.

I cannot honestly say that I had any inkling of impending horror on that seemingly ordinary afternoon, far less any sort of premonition, as I set off for the journey to my mother's home and back again, a round trip of little more than two hours. Indeed, Tom waved us off happily enough. My last sight of him living was as he closed the passenger door of my car for my mother. Then, as the car pulled away up our steep drive, I glimpsed him in the rear-view mirror, running purposefully back into the garage...

At four in the afternoon, I returned home. A damp and chilly dusk was already starting to blur the outlines on our unlit street, and I was looking forward to getting indoors and settling down cosily by the fire and the Christmas tree; perhaps to finalise those bathroom details with Tom. As usual, I operated the remote control for the up-and-over garage door and meanwhile manoeuvred my car so that I could reverse it into the left-hand bay of the double garage, glancing over my left shoulder as I did so to align the car alongside the garage wall. Then I got out of the car and turned to my right, towards the internal door leading into the house. I stopped, stricken into sudden and total immobility.

Facing me was the body of my husband, hanging from the open attic hatch in the garage.

I am not given to hysterics, but in the long moment after that initial, unfathomable shock, I screamed. That scream of horror and nightmarish disbelief echoed around the garage, but there was no one to hear, and no movement. Time slowed to an appalled and solitary stillness, as my brain struggled to take in a scene of utter ghastliness. My gaze, transfixed upwards, travelled with heart-stopping slowness from the obviously dead face, to the noose, and then onward, up along the length of rope as it disappeared into the blackness of the attic. And still my brain fought to make sense of what my eyes were witnessing. While in sickening travesty of the violent death in front of me, the vertebrae in my own neck were apparently being damaged by compression, during that unearthly pause when my life screeched to a devastating standstill, my head flung back to be locked in stunned realisation of what I was, indeed, witnessing.

Suddenly, my brain seemed to catch up with itself at last, as if in some terrible inversion of that momentary sense of déjà vu. My breathing re-started with a gasp; my body and my senses jerked simultaneously into action, as the adrenalin began to pump into my system and take over. I turned and fled.

Stumbling, running, up the steep drive; careering down the slope of the neighbouring driveway; my mind groping through its own haze of shocked disbelief to begin fearing for Angela's situation. I heard my voice, cracked and distant-sounding, ordering:

"Don't alarm her. She's just been widowed."

With a shuddering shock as I burst through her unlocked kitchen door, it dawned on me that so, too, had I.

Angela's professionalism as a nurse took over. While she was phoning 999, I slumped down at her kitchen table in an unreal state of outward calm, and silently began to question what I had just told her. Surely I must be mistaken? Some insane trick of the fading light? I could not possibly have seen that nightmare vision which I believed I had seen, and which, if true, could no longer be confined in the ominous silence of the garage but would become reality, involving others in searing agony, as well as myself.

The emergency services' telephone controllers. Calm, cool, professional, as they must invariably be. A hanging: someone must go immediately to the garage; there might still be a chance of saving him. Angela, using walking sticks while awaiting a hip replacement, could not possibly manage the steepness of Riverside's drive. So that left me. Taking Angela's mobile phone from her as I somehow forced myself upright from the chair, I noticed that my hand was shaking. The controller reiterated: I must go back. Clutching the phone like a lifeline, I ran. The police and ambulance were on their way – a few minutes only – but for those few minutes, which may as well have been hours, I would be alone. The controller was speaking as I came once more in sight of the open garage. Darkness was coming down rapidly now, but there was no mistake; no trick of the light or of the imagination. The bleak stillness of the scene which confronted me pierced me anew like an electric shock. Through the stillness came the voice of the controller:

"Can you get something to cut him down?"

"He's dead. I can't – I can't." And, silently to myself: "Don't make me."

"Are you absolutely sure he's dead? Is he cold?"

"I can't touch him. But he's dead." Then, barely above a whisper: "My husband is dead."

Unable to look any longer on that unimaginably horrific sight which I now knew was no imagining, I fled again, to pace the top of the drive and peer through the gloom for the first sign of the help I desperately needed. Around me the village was slipping into its quiet, nightly routine, while I drew in gasps of dank air and repeatedly ordered myself to remain calm.

The silence and the gloom were broken at last. Sirens wailing and lights flashing with an urgency which I already knew in my heart to be futile, two police cars and an ambulance screamed to a halt. As a policeman ran towards me, I pointed a shakily outstretched arm down the drive towards the garage. Between clenched teeth behind which I forcibly contained a rising tide of shock, I blurted out a desperate appeal against the truth, in tones which sounded strangely commanding:

"Tell me I am mistaken."

Once more I turned and fled, somehow reaching the sanctuary of Angela's kitchen. This time I flung myself down headlong at the table and dropped my head onto my pillowing arms, my eyes squeezed shut in an attempt to block out the nightmare vision for just a little longer.

And so I waited, in a state of forced and unnatural calm, for the storm which must break over me in the wake of this unthinkable tragedy, to sweep away the foundations on which my entire adult life had been built, and plunge my family and myself into churning chaos.

I didn't have long to wait. My wall of self-imposed solitude seemed suddenly to give way to a seething mass of people: a distant voice encouraging me to drink the cup of tea which was being put into my hand; another neighbour sitting beside me and holding my other hand; Angela's daughters, both nurses, materialising; women speaking in hushed tones.

Then, the door opening; men's voices. A paramedic introduced himself to Angela, gently telling her that he was one of the ambulance crew who had responded to the emergency call to attend her late husband, John, the previous week. Hearing that, though still at a great distance, seemed to galvanise my brain into some sort of action. Raising my head at last, I tried to speak clearly and firmly, addressing everyone in the room so that there could be no misunderstanding:

"Yes, that's it – *John* is the one who died, not *Tom*. It's *John* who's dead."

But as I was speaking, my voice sounding unnatural and strained even to my own ears, I became aware that I was trying to convince no one except myself. Immediately, in an act of the utmost kindness and solicitude, a policeman crouched down beside me and took my hands in his:

"Lucy: Tom is dead."

I knew then that there could be no further attempts at self-delusion. Quietly, utterly calmly, I acknowledged the full, horrific truth at last, as I replied simply:

"Yes, I know that."

I never again doubted the reality of the horror I had witnessed. And as I once more lowered my head to the comforting pillow of my arms, I heard someone, far away, saying:

"She's in deep shock."

Whether he was talking about me or not, I neither knew nor cared. But suddenly, I cared desperately for my mother, who would be worrying because I hadn't phoned, as was my invariable custom, to tell her I was home. I raised my head, concern for my family breaking through my stupor. How could I possibly break this appalling and shocking news, and by phone? My sons, too, must now be given the most devastating news imaginable; that their strong, capable father, their role model, was not only dead, but was dead by suicide. Mark in the north of the country, Paul in the southwest. Each one out of the physical reach of the comfort which they, and I, would need as never before. Someone must be with each of my sons, and my mother, when the news burst upon them.

I appealed to the nearest police officer, who assured me that arrangements would be made immediately, to send officers to my mother and to each of my sons. My first overriding concern was to ensure that the arrival of the police on her doorstep would not cause my mother to think, however momentarily, that I had been involved in a car crash on my way home. I particularly asked that on my mother opening her door, the police should tell her at once:

"Your daughter is alright."

Unfortunately it seems that message never actually got through to the officers concerned. But, in whatever way this most appalling of news was to be broken, the time had come to begin the terrible, soul-wrenching process of unleashing my waking nightmare upon the remaining people dearest to me.

Chapter 4: Speaking the unspeakable

Meanwhile, some forty miles away, my mother had long since closed the door behind me and glanced at the clock. Hopefully the return journey wouldn't take more than an hour, at the most; she'd appreciated that I'd wanted to get straight home, before the weather and the traffic worsened, and of course, I'd always been so punctilious about phoning as soon as I arrived home. As she sat down with a very welcome cup of tea, my mother reflected contentedly on another warmly enjoyable family Christmas.

She emptied her small case, put away her clothes and toiletries, and set out her Christmas presents on the coffee table, alongside her cheerful little Christmas tree, to be admired and enjoyed all over again.

Time went on. There must be some sort of delay on the roads, she realised – hardly surprising, really, with the post-Christmas sales already luring people back out to the shopping centres in their droves. But, after two hours, the nagging doubt which had crept into my mother's mind could no longer be ignored. Slightly impatient with herself for fussing, she nevertheless phoned my home number, to be answered by the usual voicemail message. Carefully replacing the receiver, my mother knew now that she was not fussing. With Tom not there to answer the phone either, something must be wrong. The obvious conclusion was that I had, indeed, been involved in an accident, and that Tom had gone straight to the hospital. Tom was always so considerate towards his mother-in-law, and of course he would let her know as soon as he had news. She would simply have to wait for his call: there was nothing else she could do.

Another cup of tea, if only to pass the time. As she was sitting down to drink it, there came every parent's worst nightmare while waiting for news of a delayed journey: a knock at the door. Jerking to her feet, spilling the tea, she breathed deeply and told herself to be calm, as she moved towards the front door. She opened it to find two seemingly huge police officers, with grave faces. Unfortunately, my request for immediate reassurance about me had been ignored.

"Mrs Allenshaw? May we come in?"

So this was it – this was how it felt. Numbing, unreal.

"Please sit down, Mrs Allenshaw."

Doing so, she took a steadying breath and asked:

"Is this about my daughter?"

"Mrs Allenshaw, we have to tell you that your son-in-law died this afternoon."

My mother, maintaining that external calm at which the women of her generation excel through sustained practice, drew a long, stunned breath and asked whether it had been a heart attack? After all, she had seen Tom just a few hours ago, at which time he had seemed fine. The police could tell her nothing more: she would have to phone me.

At about the same time, two constables from the Devon & Cornwall police were driving their car onto the crunching, frozen mud of a remote farmyard. Knocking at the farmhouse door, they asked to speak to Paul Roberts. Meanwhile, in the north of England, their counterparts were responding to a call to send two officers to a city-centre flat, where a young man named Mark Roberts was about to enjoy a peaceful evening with Clare, his long-term girlfriend.

Paul heard the news first; but simply that his father had died that afternoon – the police could give him no details. Stunned, shocked and utterly bewildered, his instinctive reaction was to phone his brother.

As soon as Mark heard the totally uncharacteristic note of panic in his brother's voice, he knew that something was terribly wrong. Unable to take in what Paul was telling him, and breathless from the sudden shock, Mark, like his brother and his grandmother a few minutes previously, heard a knock at the door. As Clare ushered two policemen into the room, Mark felt a sickening lurch of his heart, and knew that what his brother had just told him was true. *But how?* Mark, too, was told only that his father had died that afternoon. Still clutching their phones, as if to cling onto each other as their worlds began a terrifying and soul-wrenching descent into agonised confusion, the two young men knew they must now try to phone their mother.

Back in her flat, my own mother had replaced the receiver and turned to the two waiting policemen. Calmly and evenly, more for her own understanding than theirs, she repeated aloud those horrifying words which I had croaked disbelievingly to her down the telephone line, though in terror of their effect on her:

"Tom has hanged himself."

One of the policemen guided her into a chair, solicitous and even alarmed. But there was no time to lose, as instinct took over: the instinct of a mother to comfort her child, however adult that child may now be.

"I must return to my daughter immediately. Would you please phone for a cab while I re-pack my bag?"

The other officer had been speaking into his radio, and now turned to my mother.

"We'll drive you back to your daughter's house in the police car, as soon as you're ready. Please, take your time, Mrs Allenshaw, you've had a terrible shock."

But with characteristic disregard for herself, my mother could think only of her daughter – and her grandsons; did they know yet? – as she hastily re-packed the essentials for a stay which would probably be lengthy. A very short while later, she sat in the back of a police car making its way as fast as possible back to Riverside, and repeated those words in her mind, over and over:

"Tom has hanged himself."

How could this have happened? Reliable, sensible, trustworthy Tom, the bedrock of his family. But for now, at least, she could think no further than the end of this dark and unreal journey.

Back in the West Country, Paul threw aside his mobile phone as he tried to take in what I had just told him. Dad – his role model, his standard of perfection – dead? By *suicide*? This was impossible, unreal – some sort of nightmare from which he would, surely, wake up soon. Groping once more for his phone while almost blinded by sudden, hot tears, Paul called his girlfriend, hundreds of miles away with her family in Germany.

Suicide. Mark repeated the ugly word to himself as his phone fell unheeded to the floor, trying to understand what he had just heard, but failing completely. Stricken, shaking and unable to utter any sound except a half-suppressed howl of anguish, he threw himself into the sanctuary of Clare's embrace. And sobbed.

For the third time in horribly quick succession, I let my own mobile phone fall from my hand. A hellish nightmare, from which there could be no awakening, had now been unleashed and would run its devastating course, bringing the most searing pain and misery to an ever-increasing number of people.

Telling my mother had been hard enough, fearing all the while for her heart, her cancer... But immediately after that, I was required to perform the hardest task of my life so far: to inform my two sons that there was no mistake in what they had each been told; their father really was dead. And as each stricken voice in turn asked me desperately what had happened, I knew that any attempt to conceal the truth, however temporarily, would be both unfair and unkind. And so I was obliged to tell my sons, as gently as I could, that their father had committed suicide; that he had hanged himself. But in telling them, I learned that there is very limited room for gentleness, in imparting such starkly horrific news. That same instinct which was bringing my own mother back to me with the utmost urgency, tore uselessly at my heart as I forced myself to speak the unspeakable to each of my sons, all the while cursing the distances between us.

Two young men, facing one of the cruellest and most shattering blows imaginable. The potential effects on them were too catastrophic and too profound to contemplate: I was already realising that. But, for now, my only concern was to remain calm for their sakes. With one parent having deliberately and horrifically destroyed himself, the remaining one must provide sanctuary, stability and strength, despite being hundreds of miles away from the longed-for comfort of physical contact. Once Mark and Paul had each regained sufficient capacity to take in anything more than the stunning blow which I had no choice but to inflict, their very real and desperate concern for me became movingly evident. As best I could, I assured them both that I was safe in Angela's house, that their grandmother was on her way back to me, and that the emergency services had taken charge. Putting the phone down after each of those calls was unspeakable agony, but I found that my attention was being required elsewhere. For the official practicalities of death – of violent and unnatural death – were already beginning their relentless intrusion upon the personal miseries which are its brutal legacy.

The first to claim my attention as I struggled to surface from my initial, overwhelming shock, was a detective sergeant who introduced himself very courteously, and then proceeded to inform me that he was "in charge of the case."

While he continued speaking I found my fragile attention wandering, as I struggled to reconcile the shock of my too-recent discovery in the garage, with the well-practised routine of officialdom in converting a personal catastrophe into a properly documented 'case'. I was informed that my house had been sealed off by the police, and would remain so until the coroner's official, now on the premises, had completed her investigations alongside the police team. I remembered my dog, still in the house, and asked if she could be brought to me. No: not while the entire premises remained under investigation.

Too deeply shocked to contemplate the absurdity of such bureaucratic overkill – and I make no apology for using that particular term – I responded automatically to the flow of questions about my movements that afternoon. My account would need to be confirmed by my mother, apparently.

My mother! The sound of a car on the drive; a door opening; then she and I were holding each other, in a degree of shock and a mutual comfort too profound for any words. Eyes wide with horror as we supported each other to Angela's sofa, we each scrutinised the other's ashen face with an unprecedented level of concern.

Endless cups of tea – that staunchest of allies and time-honoured remedy for shock – were being put into our hands as we tried to make ourselves understand that the unimaginable had actually happened. This was not some ludicrously overstated work of fiction, but our own hideous new reality.

Next to arrive in Angela's sitting room, which in my increasingly feverish mind seemed to be overwhelmingly crowded, was the coroner's official. Through the haze of shock which was enveloping me in a muffling mistiness, I registered mild surprise at her being quite young and well-dressed, and wondered vaguely how such a person came to do a job which must, surely, be invariably sordid. But these faraway contemplations were brought to an abrupt halt as, with the preliminaries over, she told me that there was a suicide note; did I wish to see it now? My mother and I shook our heads in unison. But there was 'another letter' addressed to me personally, which the police had extracted from my husband's briefcase and which was now in this official's possession. No, I most emphatically did not wish to see that now, either. Mercifully, at that point I could have no idea of the use to which that letter would later be put, by officialdom intent on finding a convenient reason for a cataclysmic action.

My phone rang again. It was Mark, to tell me Clare and her mother would drive him down from the north the following day. Though the words were tumbling over each other in his shock, the prospect of real, solid action brought the first merest hint of comfort to us both.

Mark's call was followed immediately by Paul's, to say he, too, would arrive the next day, but he would be driving himself up from the West Country. My very real concern at the idea of his driving such a distance, alone and so soon after such a massive shock, was swiftly and peremptorily swept aside. Already, my younger son was displaying a forerunner of that anger against his father which would, in the months to come, consume us both. But for now, his promise of at least trying to sleep, and of then driving with the utmost care, would have to suffice. Clearly he, too, simply needed to be here, to give and receive some sort of comfort. And so the first tiny pinpricks of light would appear, tomorrow, in the encircling darkness in which we were all floundering.

I turned my attention back to the hum of voices, as best I could. Arrangements were being made; I would need to attend the coroner's office on the next working day, which would be New Year's Eve. I nodded mechanically, reacting to each fresh piece of information like an automaton. And still the room seemed to fill with yet more people, as various police officers and ambulance crew came and went. Finally the room began to empty, with a flurry of handshakes and giving of business cards.

Suddenly there was a well-known sound of approach, as my dog barked out her relief on joining me at last. I scooped her up, and buried my face in her soft, living warmth: the sole, silent witness of my husband's final preparations for the ending of his life. I held her close.

Much later, I lay beside my mother in Angela's spare bed, in the silence of the longest night I had ever known. I was still wearing the clothes I had worn throughout that endless and life-changing day. None of us had given any thought to Angela's daughter collecting anything else from the house other than my dog and her bed: such everyday matters belonged to a world which, for us, was now held in ghastly suspension, a normality once-removed. I repeated those words over and over again in my head, trying to make sense of them:

"Tom is dead."

Whether my eyes were open or closed made no difference to the horror of the vision which was constantly in front of them. In her bed on the floor beside me, Misty slept peacefully. My mother and I did not. From time to time, one or the other of us would whisper tentatively into the dark:

"Are you awake?"

To which the response was invariably:

"Yes."

The seemingly interminable night wore on, until finally, at almost five in the morning, the sound of a car heralded the arrival of the duty doctor, whose visit to my mother and myself had been requested by the ambulance crew some twelve hours previously. Not, perhaps, the NHS response we might have hoped for (had we had the capacity to think about it), given the circumstances and my mother's age and illness. But, courteous and concerned, the doctor apologised for the delay: the winter-sickness bug was rife in the neighbourhood. I wished fervently that we could exchange our heart-sickness for mere winter-sickness. Blood pressure, heart rate, all fine in both our cases, surprisingly, but the doctor emphasised that we must both be seen at the surgery as soon as possible: we were going to need help to get through this.

Chapter 5: Return to abnormality

Walking back down our own – *my* own – drive, the following morning, had a trance-like quality of unreality, rather as though I were gliding light-headedly onto a stage set. Except that I had no idea of how this scene was supposed to be played out, and I was almost senseless with foreboding as I tried to come to terms with my own inescapable part in it. I had been thrust both mentally and physically into a new and utterly alien world; a world in which I had completely lost control of my situation and no longer understood my own role. A world with rules and demands as yet unknown to me, which would have terrified me had I not been too deeply sunk in shock even to begin to contemplate them.

Doing my best to ignore the now-closed garage door, and the horror so recently and vividly present on the other side of it, I forced myself to focus on my immediate and visible surroundings, which I seemed to be viewing through some sort of telescopic tube. Everything around me felt remote and untouchable, as though even our physical possessions had been frozen into unreality, in that moment when my entire world had lurched seismically, to assume a new and distorted shape. Our house appeared utterly familiar and yet shockingly different; altered far beyond my dazed recognition. I concentrated on helping my mother over the high front doorstep, my face turned away from the festive decoration on the front door, which had suddenly become, to me, not a Christmas wreath but a mourning wreath.

Inescapably, Tom's study was first to come into view as we entered the hall, its door standing wide open. I gazed uncomprehendingly at the post-it notes, papers and mobile phones still scattered over his two desks, as if they were waiting, poised for his imminent return and a smooth continuation of his normal routine. But something seemed vaguely wrong or out of place: in that long, slow moment of looking at Tom's perfectly ordinary workplace, I noticed that neither of his laptops was there. I concluded, dazedly, that the police must have taken them away for examination. Then, forcing myself onward, I walked past our sitting room doorway, which revealed the full-height

Christmas tree chosen by Tom and myself with such pleasure so very recently. One or two opened presents were still lying on the floor. Then into the kitchen, and automatically filling the kettle to make yet more tea.

Yet more tea would become a constant necessity, because now there was more pain to inflict, as I steeled myself to begin the task of phoning my husband's – my *late* husband's – relatives and boss. Each phone call seemed even more unreal than the last, as I tried to break the unthinkable news as gently as I could. Already, I felt as if I were relating a story; this must be something which was happening to someone else. But concentrating on other people's inevitable pain provided a focus for my thoughts and my words, and prevented me thinking too much on my own account. I had already learned, though, when telling my sons, that there is no gentle way to impart the news of sudden, violent death – particularly when it has been self-inflicted.

People's reactions to such intense trauma vary, naturally, according to temperament, and that day I ran the entire gamut of emotional outpourings, from the deepest concern for my sons and myself, to outright disbelief, to an outburst of anger accompanied by an insistence that the family member I had just informed was the main person affected, and was already suffering far more than anyone else, including myself. I half-listened to this particular relative's lengthy tirade, staring fixedly through the decorated branches of the Christmas tree towards the bleak, wintry garden beyond. I wished heartily that the shining festive symbol weren't there, seeming silently to mock me...

It wasn't there for long, actually. The news had already begun to spread through the village, and people were starting to arrive. A neighbour brought soup for our lunch; someone gave me a homeopathic calming remedy; someone else took the dog for a walk. By the afternoon a casserole dish containing our dinner had arrived, and several people were at work silently removing the decorations from the Christmas tree, which had turned from a symbol of joy and hope into a sickening aberration. And in between thanking people for their visits (as best I could), I continued with that seemingly-endless stream of phone calls.

31

Despite the limitless flow of hot, comforting tea, my throat was already beginning to hurt from the constant need to talk. By now utterly devoid of sense, feeling or appetite, I nevertheless turned to the soup, eventually, with relief; if only for the sake of my throat.

The day wore on. By now I was functioning purely on auto-pilot, my own feelings submerged beneath the engulfing tide of other people's emotional needs. I almost felt as though I should apologise for inflicting this on them; as though perhaps it could somehow be my fault. At some stage my brother arrived, pale with shock and unable to speak as he enveloped me in his arms in an attempt to comfort me. Then there followed the agony of waiting for my sons to arrive.

Paul, on the farm, remained true to his earlier insistence that he would drive himself back to me, only two days after he had left in such good spirits. His voice, as I listened to him again on the phone that morning, sounded noticeably calmer and more determined, as he outlined his plans and reassured me that he had, somehow, slept. I realised that this responsibility to get himself here in safety would actually provide an outlet of emotion for this practical young man of action. I accepted his assurances with a calmness which I was determined would match his own, as I realised that I had no choice but to trust my adult son's judgment. But the relief, as his car pulled onto the drive in the late afternoon, caused me to choke back a sob as I ran to meet him. His eyes bloodshot with tiredness in a face taut and drawn, his answering sob burst out, finally, on that single word which was to haunt us all in the long months ahead:

"*Why?*"

In response I could only hold him to me, both of us shaking and breathless in our shared disbelief.

Shortly afterwards, at dusk, another set of headlights shone down the drive; peering out into the gloom, I realised that Mark had arrived, with Clare and her mother. The agony of a nightmarish journey was etched on Mark's face, too, as he in turn ran stumbling towards me. In a silence broken only by the escape of his first, anguished sob, we held each other in the gathering darkness.

Physical needs, first; hot drinks, warmth, bodily closeness. Clare constantly at Mark's side. Her mother, who had concentrated – despite her own shock – on safely negotiating an eight-hour drive, now showing concern only for Mark, Paul, my mother and me. But she had already realised, of course, that her daughter would share fully in my son's agony, and therefore her whole family must inevitably be drawn into this nightmare, as the ripples began to spread out from that unfathomable pool of despair. Despair which, a little over twenty-four hours previously, none of us had known existed.

At the sight of Mark's ashen face, stricken with the same unbearable grief written so plainly on his brother's, I suppose it was pure maternal instinct which took over; the desire to shield and protect my children as far as possible. But as my two sons and I clung to each other, standing there in the hall, I heard and felt the anguished, shuddering howl of each of them for his father. As that desolate sound tore into what was left of my own heart, I too, like Paul the previous day, felt the first stirrings of an unknown and terrible emotion. It would grow to become, eventually, anger towards the man who could inflict such a lifelong wound on his own children. Because, standing there and feeling my sons' six-foot-tall frames wracked by choking, devastating emotion, I already knew that their lives, along with my own, had been irrevocably changed; blighted and damaged to an extent as yet unknown. All peace of mind was gone, and whether that in itself could ever be regained, I could not yet begin to contemplate.

That evening passed in a haze of unreality. The family together again, and yet not together. The casserole eaten but not tasted. My mother's relief at seeing her grandsons, but her pain on my behalf compounded by her pain on theirs. Beds made up, but sleep still seemingly impossible.

The next day, New Year's Eve, was a Monday: to everyone else, either a continuation of the winter holiday, or just a normal working day. And that, for me, meant the pre-arranged appointment with the coroner's official, at an office situated within a complex housing the area's main police station and the Crown Court. But that would not be until after my mother and I

33

had first been checked by my doctor; an immediate appointment had been arranged when I had phoned that morning. Thankfully I'd had little explaining to do by phone, as the emergency doctor's report had already been received and acted on by the surgery.

Clearly, the surgery's reception staff had been forewarned of our arrival, and of our need; ushering us gently, obtaining my mother's details as a 'temporary patient', as quietly and unobtrusively as possible. Then to the doctor's consulting room: his own eyes wide with shock, his manner unflappably kind but unmistakably horrified. Checking blood pressure; prescribing a mild sedative; telling me what to expect at the coroner's office that afternoon. And, already, able to tell me that his staff had searched thoroughly right through my late husband's medical records, back as far as childhood, looking for any clue; some indication of depressive tendencies. There was none.

I was, of course, totally unfit to drive, and probably physically incapable of actually doing so. More importantly, I could not possibly even begin to think of entering the garage, either from the drive or from the house. Not for some long time yet. My family were appalled that I'd even mentioned driving, however tentatively; my brother assured me immediately that he would take me to the police station in his car, while Mark and Paul, who had clearly discussed the forthcoming meeting, were both insistent on accompanying me. I was relieved at their unequivocal decision, despite my fear for the additional pain that the experience might inflict on them. The appointment was for three o'clock; by the time this particular ordeal was over, the winter afternoon would already be closing in. We braced ourselves as best we could.

As my sons and I were being driven into the town by my brother, I stared uncomprehendingly at the mid-afternoon bustle, bewildered and even offended that the rest of the world should be going about its business as normal, and even preparing for the annual turn-of-the-year party. As if nothing had happened.

The police station was as bleak and featureless as such places usually are. A few hard, plastic chairs in the waiting area; a few advisory and cautionary posters adorning the otherwise blank walls; a bored-looking young woman on duty, telling us to wait. Then the coroner's official, whom I recognised as having been present in Angela's house and in charge of mine, emerging from behind a scuffed and uninviting door to announce that she needed to see me alone, first; without my sons. As I rose to follow her I was surprised and annoyed to feel that my legs seemed to be shaking. Seated on another hard plastic chair in front of the official's desk, I was now informed of the reason for my solitary interview. In addition to the suicide note, which my sons and I would see shortly, there was another document being regarded as 'evidence', which the police had removed from my husband's briefcase. It was this document which I was now required to read and to comment upon. In an atmosphere becoming steadily more ominous, a single sheet of A4 paper was produced and handed to me.

I took it with a sense of chill foreboding, and was horrified to find myself staring at a letter in my husband's own handwriting, addressed to me, but which I had never seen before. The letter was undated, but from its subject, I knew immediately that it had been written three years earlier. I could be absolutely certain of its date, because the subject was the most serious disagreement, amounting in fact to a row, which Tom and I had ever had. Its contents were a restatement of Tom's viewpoint in that row, concluding with an evidently heartfelt declaration of his ongoing love for me. All this was in the wake of an event which actually amounted to no more than a commonplace marital tiff: a row over money. The subject of the disagreement had been Tom's apparently sudden desire to transfer our marital home into the names of our sons, to gain some particular taxation advantage. I had refused my consent, largely due to the complications which would arise whenever our sons should eventually buy their own homes, but also because I felt it simply was not a wise or sensible action to take. From the tone of the letter, I knew it must have been written immediately after that row but, for some reason known only to Tom, it had never left his own possession, but remained in his briefcase.

There was absolutely nothing in that three-year-old letter to imply that Tom would eventually go on to develop suicidal thoughts. The police and the coroner's official, on the other hand, clearly held very different views. They had already decided that, being undated and found in his current briefcase, the letter must have been written shortly before my husband killed himself, and so must have a direct bearing on his suicide, despite its containing no reference whatsoever to any such thoughts. In other words, it implicated the row, and therefore myself, as a cause of my husband's decision to commit suicide.

Struggling to pull my thoughts together while silently ordering myself to remain calm, I informed this official of State that my husband kept many old documents in his study and, evidently, in his briefcase; that, in fact, he never threw anything away. My assertion was met with a blank silence.

Still reeling from this latest shock, I became aware of my sons being ushered into the interview room. The suicide note was produced, in its sealed 'Evidence' bag. Mark, Paul and I drew close together. As we read, scarcely able to believe the cruelty of the words, we huddled closer still, as though each of us would try to protect the others. The words seared into my consciousness. False impressions warped into vicious accusations, facts twisted out of all recognition, by a mind in which all reasoning power, all normality, had obviously been switched off. In his demented quest to lay the blame for his suicide anywhere except on his own failure to seek help, my husband had lashed out in several directions – but principally in mine.

His suicide note, typed and signed in a sickeningly business-like fashion, contained no apology for his action or any hint of regret at the pain it would cause. On the contrary, the chillingly inverted logic underlying his words indicated that he viewed his decision to commit suicide as a perfectly rational and well considered one, just as though he were making an executive decision at work. Tom's resentment and sense of isolation were, he had decided, due principally to my own increasing independence, confidence and sociability in our new life, which seemed to him symptomatic of the wider family's diminishing reliance on him. He had come to believe himself totally and deliberately excluded. Consequently, he had lost his sense of self-worth and his perception of his place within his family –

along with his reason. Ever the perfectionist, Tom had then proceeded to assess our marriage according to the same measure he had always used to assess everything else in his life. Falling short of absolute perfection by one notch had precisely the same effect as falling short by ten notches, or even by a hundred notches: it still meant falling short. By this measure, then, my husband addressed me for the final time in his suicide note, with the words:

"I wish we could have been happier."

There was no assertion that 'this is the only way', which so often seems to be associated with the final outpouring of a suicidal mind; or perhaps the only outpouring, as in this case. But Tom's last words to me were simply a statement of the facts as he had by then come to see them. Facts so grotesquely warped that he must have been viewing them as if in a series of distorting mirrors at some sort of insanely whirling and chaotic fairground, where nothing is as it seems, and the voice of reason has already been drowned in a hideous, mocking cacophony.

But as I sat in that bleak, forbidding office, staring at the cellophane-encased note with its official 'Evidence' label, my own mind was very far from considering what had been going on inside my husband's mind, as he was writing those hurtful words. I could only focus on the fact that his lifelong penchant for sulking, for disdaining all discussion, and for insisting on having the last word at whatever cost, all came together here, in this one act of brutal finality. Accusations which, however outrageously untrue, were being taken perfectly seriously by the police and which, even more importantly to my shattered family, were in any case guaranteed to wound their innocent victims. His words were going to remain imprinted on our hearts – like an angry, ugly scar – for the rest of our lives: of that I was already in no doubt. Such, I told myself bitterly, was the legacy of this husband and father to his family.

The coroner's official was speaking once again. During their investigation of the premises, the police had even gone through the contents of the paper shredder in my husband's study, from which they had recovered at least one previous draft of the suicide note. This was currently under investigation. *Why?* I wondered. Surely it was obvious: Tom had suffered some catastrophic mental breakdown which had resulted in his decision to take his own life. Apparently, though, the police did not regard it as being quite so straightforward: the coroner's official now informed me that a full written statement would be required from me, as part of the investigation into my husband's unexplained death. My statement would then be submitted to the coroner for his consideration prior to the inquest.

So the next stage, in this seemingly relentless flow of official inquisition, was to be the taking of that formal statement by a detective constable, who would contact me to arrange a time and date to interview me at home. *Interview – or interrogate?* I wondered with the first tinge of bitterness, through the haze of shock which seemed only to have increased during the forty-eight hours since my discovery of my husband's body.

And so began my chill realisation that suicide has unforeseen and unimagined consequences, in addition to the intended ones. Those consequences were already gathering momentum, to wreak relentless havoc as they reached out ever more widely from the silent, dark and tormented hinterland which had been the suicidal mind of my husband.

Chapter 6: Unholy crisis

Stumbling, clinging to each other in our genuine need of physical support, the three of us rejoined my brother in the waiting area. Having taken one look at our faces, he wordlessly guided us to his car. We all endured the homeward journey, through the rain and the gloom, in silence. But even as I was dragging myself indoors from the car, I was met by the next twist in this truly unholy crisis: walking towards us down the drive was a man in a clerical dog-collar, who proceeded to introduce himself to my brother as *Father* Someone-or-other.

Apparently, a devoutly Catholic neighbour had decided that what I needed at this particular time was her parish priest. While this was evidently well-meant, in my view it was actually misguided, inappropriate and even interfering. Peremptorily, I asked my brother to inform the reverend gentleman that I was in no fit state to see anyone. As I climbed the stairs to seek my own personal version of sanctuary, in my bed, I was struck by the first moment of irony in this unfolding nightmare. A *Catholic* priest: didn't they preach, until comparatively recently, that a suicide is condemned to eternal damnation, having committed the one unforgivable sin? As I closed my bedroom door against the world, I found myself shaking, and fell to my knees: not from any religious fervour, but simply from the accumulated effects of shock. I crawled across the room to my bed, longing for its enveloping comfort, and its promise of protection from a world whose foundations were slithering and shifting beneath me like the aftershocks of a massive earthquake.

My mother was already lying down; my sons now softly closed the door of the room they were sharing. I hoped they would escape into their own private world, however temporarily, as they had always done during childhood and teenage crises, and yet how minor those crises must seem to them now. My brother brought me tea, hot and welcome. But Tom's suicide note, and the undated letter with its implications too terrible to contemplate, had destroyed the last of my strength. For the time being, at least.

That night I was ill. Just vomiting and giddiness, no doubt due to the layer upon layer of shock, but Mark and Paul, already with enough agony of their own to bear, were sufficiently worried to call out a doctor to me, early the next morning. I was by then not even capable of getting out of bed, let alone getting to the surgery. How I hated being an additional burden to my suffering family, but my entire system – physical, mental and emotional – was evidently at overload, and could take on no more.

Unfortunately, though, there was still plenty more to be taken on. It would simply have to wait, for a short while at least, as the depth of the initial shock, compounded by the continuing after-shocks, took an increasing toll. I had no choice but to spend the next day in bed, though all the time feeling desperately guilty at leaving the rest of my grief-stricken family to get on with fielding the endless phone calls and visits. But a day spent essentially alone with my own private grief, even though it inevitably included my own private torture, must have restored my strength, to some extent at least. That day, I realised afterwards, must have been New Year's Day, but as a family we didn't even notice.

Huddled under the duvet, I shivered uncontrollably as my brain feverishly sought to reconcile the hideous and utterly hellish vision of Tom dead, with the ordinary and apparently happy vision of Tom alive, as we enjoyed post-Christmas drinks with a neighbouring couple, less than twenty-four hours before Tom hanged himself. That innocuous and apparently relaxed evening now belonged in another, unreachably normal world, peopled by a normal family enjoying a warm Christmastime evening with friends, and looking forward to a normal, optimistic New Year. But as that restless day wore on, I formed my own resolutions, which had nothing to do with the New Year: they were simply to recover at least some of my strength as quickly as possible, enabling me to reassure my family that I was not really ill, and to get on with learning how to handle this ghastly situation. Those resolutions would need to stay with me during the long months to come.

The remainder of the family decided to ignore the phone that day, and turn callers away, on the grounds that I was ill and needed absolute quiet. The unaccustomed peace in the house that day did us all good, and with me in bed, my sons and their grandmother had a much-needed opportunity to draw breath and to concentrate on supporting each other.

The following day I managed to stir myself into action, more or less normally. I had no choice, since Mark and his companions would need to leave again that morning. My elder son was utterly devastated at leaving me to face the consequences of his father's actions without him. Now, though, I began to feel my strength rising, as I strove to set Mark's mind at rest on my account, and to alleviate his own suffering as best I could. But his white face, with agonised eyes staring from the rain-soaked window of the car as it pulled away, was quite simply a study in misery.

Next to leave was my brother, but with the promise of returning in a day or two. Meanwhile Paul was taking a brief nap before his own, reluctant return journey to the West Country. As he left, neighbours were coming and going; bringing further gifts of food, walking the dog, just wanting to check on me. They evidently needed to be doing something to help, however small, with their shock and their pain for me written on their faces. By the time they'd all left, and the phone had finally stopped ringing for the evening, my voice was once again hoarse.

But now my mother and I were alone, and so we could concentrate on helping each other. My mother was already proving her determination to weather this crisis and to see me safely through it, showing a capability, stamina and sheer force of character which belied her eighty-nine years, not to mention her own ongoing battle with cancer. With so many people in the house, she and I had been sharing my bed – the bed I used to share with my husband – but now the time seemed right for her to move back into the room she usually occupied.

As I lay down alone that night and closed my eyes, trying to force away the hellish vision which inevitably rose behind my closed lids, I knew this was my first, minute step towards independence, and therefore towards my eventual recovery.

The next couple of days passed in a haze of neighbours, phone calls and, crucially, appointments. A neighbour drove me to the doctor, who exhibited the same gentle concern as on my previous visit, but decided to increase the sedative dosage. Next was the funeral director, who outlined initial arrangements in an atmosphere of warmth and calm while I drank tea and made preliminary notes. I found note-taking incredibly helpful during each of those early and terrifyingly unknown situations; it seemed to prevent the awful sensation of floundering, while also helping me to begin to address my situation and, therefore, to understand the actions I needed to take.

It was becoming increasingly apparent that my personal and financial crises were going to intensify in the aftermath of the initial devastation. But one of the earliest shafts of light in the darkness came when, at the recommendation of a friend, I asked a local and highly-regarded solicitor to call on me at home. This senior partner in the firm was clearly very experienced, and possessed a manner which at once calmed some of my worst fears and inspired confidence. By the time he left after our initial meeting, his car weighed down by the volume of papers which he and I had removed from my husband's study, I was almost overwhelmed by the relief of knowing that I would not face the business and financial consequences completely alone.

During the ordeal of the following months, as I dealt with the endless and heartless obstacles engineered by sundry officials of State, business and financial institutions, I would come to rely on the professional advice of various members of this firm of solicitors. Along with my family and close friends, I referred to them as a vital part of my 'support team'. They were able to offer me invaluable support as their knowledge grew, not only of my circumstances, but also of my character. Initially, though, as I introduced the senior partner to my mother at the end of that first meeting, she shook his hand warmly as she assured him that:

"My daughter looks better already."

Sadly, that improvement was not destined to last. In their zeal to help, or at least to offer comfort and support, people have a tendency to outstay their welcome, however inadvertently, and whether in person or by phone. Of course I appreciated all the concern, support and offers of help, but I found that it could be extremely wearing at times, particularly when accompanied by long and involved stories of how they had felt when various members of their own family died. Not, however, by suicide: so the assurances that people 'knew how I felt' sounded at best, hollow, and at worst, irritating. But everyone was invariably so kind and concerned that it would have seemed the height of discourtesy to ask them to leave, or to interrupt in order to bring a lengthy phone call to an abrupt end. And anyway, I didn't seem to have the strength left to do that. And so I would listen in silence, and occasionally nod across the room or murmur into the phone, all the time longing to be alone for a while with my thoughts, however ghastly those thoughts might be.

Meanwhile various relatives of Tom's had also begun to phone, having at least absorbed the initial blow of the news I had given them on the day after his death. Two sets of his relatives now announced their joint arrival the following day. Bracing myself, I responded with as much courtesy as I could muster, even though I was in fact being told, rather than asked, to provide hospitality. After all, I reasoned, these people are Tom's family, and they must be suffering from varying degrees of shock themselves, although I felt that particular consideration did not wholly excuse their peremptory attitude towards me.

By Friday evening I had no voice left at all, merely from the constant talking. I could feel that my brief improvement had quite simply evaporated, to the consternation of my already cruelly tormented mother. But far worse was to come.

Chapter 7: Relative values

The invasion began on the following morning. It was now a week since the start of this ongoing nightmare, and although I found myself performing all the necessary and everyday tasks like an automaton, I was probably in a more profound state of shock than I had been in the initial stages, as the full implications continued to force their way into my numbed consciousness. But before I could deal with Tom's family, I knew that I could no longer delay informing my own friends, now geographically very widespread.

Email seems a very impersonal method of communication, particularly for such a horrific piece of news as I had to give, but a draft email is so easy to amend, of course, and very efficient. So, at six o'clock that morning I was sitting up in bed, my laptop on my knees and the inevitable cup of tea beside me, writing something which, were it not for the agonising pain inside me, even I would have thought must be pure fiction. In fact, on reading the first few lines, one of my lifelong friends initially thought it couldn't possibly be true, but must be a plotline for a new story. By eight o'clock my message had been sent, and by midday the deeply shocked and equally deeply concerned replies had started to arrive.

Unfortunately I didn't have much time to read them, as Tom's relatives had also started to arrive, and were evidently expecting lunch. But in the midst of the chaos came the most welcome arrival possible; Paul, returned yet again from the farm, with his boss's blessing. Paul's German girlfriend, Bea – they'd only been together a few weeks – had been at home with her family for Christmas, but on hearing the news by phone from a distraught Paul, with *her* family's blessing she had made immediate arrangements to fly to London, to offer support to her new boyfriend and his family. Paul would be taken by our local taxi driver to meet her that evening. In the meantime, practical as ever, he scooped up sundry relatives, matched them as nearly as possible to our stock of Wellington boots (the females of the 'party', at least, certainly not having arrived prepared for a country walk), and bore them off with Misty. He then collected

Angela's dog and walked them all, relatives and dogs alike, around the fields behind the house for as long as possible, or at least until good manners dictated that the relatives' mounting complaints could no longer be ignored. Meanwhile my brother set off for the village shop, so that he, my mother and I could then prepare a lunch of cheese, cold meat and salad. To me, it felt as monumental a task as the feeding of the five thousand.

Grief must surely be one of the most powerful human emotions, and perhaps never more so than when it comes out of nowhere to strike with sudden, devastating force; the effect being remarkably similar to that of being stunned by a massive physical blow. In the case of suicide, the after-effects tend to warp the truth about the normal relationships which have been brought to such an abrupt end. The result is almost a parody of the warped truth inside the mind of that person who stood on the brink of destroying his own life, and with it his entire family's peace of mind.

This, at least, appeared to be true in the case of one particular relative of Tom's, whose greeting was to inform me in high-handed tones that, as he'd already told me by phone, his grief was far harder to bear than mine could possibly be, simply because he'd known Tom from birth. Too numb to deal effectively with such a crass assertion, I rather curtly reminded him that I had discovered my husband's hanged body. This consideration was instantly swept aside as being a mere nothing, with a loud and brash assurance that this particular relative had seen far worse sights than *that*.

I stood up, shakily, and left the room. Finally allowing the hot, angry tears to flow in private as I sat alone in my study, I realised that I would have to steel myself to deal with such people, during the coming months. It was becoming unnervingly apparent that not only was my own and my family's ordeal nowhere near over: it had scarcely begun.

Paul's head appeared tentatively round the door: a little spot of colour in each otherwise-pale cheek, he told me that he and the taxi driver were about to leave for the airport. Hastily drying my own cheeks, I hugged him and asked him to assure Bea that she would be warmly welcomed, despite our circumstances. After all, it seemed to me that the poor girl was travelling on a hastily-arranged mission of mercy, to place herself among people she'd never met, in a foreign country, and in a suddenly blighted household which could easily turn out to be the most appalling house of horrors. Her parents had made her travel arrangements while she packed, and then driven her to the airport. I liked the entire family already.

My mother was resting in her room after lunch. More neighbours arrived, giving me an excuse to leave my relatives-in-law in the sitting room, consuming tea and biscuits and speculating on Tom's motives, while I 'received' my other callers upstairs in my study. I was quickly learning to love that small, enclosing room, as it became my own private sanctuary from the world. Everything was there: my old and well-worn desk, my familiar books and photos, and my electric 'stove' throwing out light, warmth and comfort. A guest and I could flop onto the old and well-worn sofa bed, which had been transported so cheerfully by Tom and myself up Riverside's tight-cornered staircase. That had been no mean feat in itself, as the bed mechanism had suddenly sprung open partway up the stairs, threatening unceremoniously to deposit a section of the banisters, plus the sofa bed with me still attached, into the grandfather clock's waiting hands (as it were) in the hall below. Happy memories; and so, perhaps, a fitting place to begin trying to take in what had happened to my family and to me.

Standing once again on the drive in the gathering dusk, I watched as Paul got out of the taxi, moving swiftly round to open the door for a tall, blonde girl who bore an air of quiet confidence but an expression of the deepest concern. There was no need of words in any language, as I moved forward with open arms and she ran to me. As we held each other, in mutual agony for the trauma inflicted on a young man for whom we were each desperately concerned, I sensed that in Bea, Paul had found someone with strength and resourcefulness to match his own. I was deeply relieved: he and Mark were going to need all the support they could get.

Tom's relatives were gone, for that evening at least. The next need was a hot meal for the rest of us; a family meal, but without the head of the family. Paul clearly couldn't bear to take his father's place opposite me. Everyone made the effort to converse, as normally as we could, but I noticed that all eyes remained averted from the empty place at the head of the table.

But what of the effects of all this on my eighty-nine year old mother? She was already five years into her own, intensely private trauma: her battle with cancer. With the calm stoicism of the women of her generation and type, she was rising to this challenge as she had risen to all the others. Her values are perhaps best summed up by that now-famous slogan, which first appeared on a poster prepared but never used during the Second World War, and now spawned on countless t-shirts, shopping bags and coffee mugs: *Keep calm and carry on*. Deal with the practicalities; hold the family together; offer genuine but never intrusive emotional support. She was proving herself to be this devastated family's true matriarch, in the best and noblest sense of the word.

Knowing that those same relatives of Tom's would return the next day, I had placed an online grocery order. As we sat down to our family meal, the phone rang: my order could not be delivered, because the credit card payment had been refused. I rang the credit card company immediately, to be told that my husband had placed a 'stop' on our joint credit cards a week previously: on the day of his death. Quietly, I took my mother aside. Even before I had finished speaking, she was reaching into her handbag for her own credit card. The grocery order was saved.

By coincidence, the following morning I received the statement for that joint credit card account, which showed a perfectly normal balance owing. For the first time since my husband's death, I now logged on to my computer to view our financial accounts. Both the current account, and the savings account from which the credit card bill had always been paid, showed a nil balance. All funds had been withdrawn on the day of Tom's death. Aghast and shaking, I telephoned my solicitor as soon as his office was open. In the absence of my husband's computer, it was taking his team longer to establish the details, but they were already hard at work tracking down the missing funds. My solicitor, as the partner now in overall charge of my affairs, was confident of their eventual success and advised me to try not to worry too much about the interim practicalities.

My instinctive reaction was to inform my mother of this latest blow, which I did immediately. True to form, she assured me that if Paul would drive her to the nearest cash machine, she would withdraw sufficient cash to keep me afloat once I was alone. Because, as I already knew, she needed to be driven home that evening by my brother, ready for a hospital appointment the following day: cancer waits for no man, or woman, whatever other tragedies he or she may be enduring at the time.

But the underlying fact of my financial crisis was profoundly disturbing: *why* would Tom have induced this extra agony for me to handle, in addition to the far greater one of his suicide? Unless, of course, this turned out to be only part of a greater financial intrigue, involving a darker purpose than mere vindictiveness towards me. If so, the full details would no doubt be revealed by the ongoing investigation into his financial affairs. Meanwhile, I could only try to reassure myself that he had merely viewed the transfer of our money out of my reach, with the same warped sense of business logic with which he had viewed his decision to commit suicide.

Keep calm and carry on. Now I found myself repeating that phrase like a mantra, clinging to it while my safe, ordered world continued its very real disintegration. The day followed the same nightmarish pattern as the previous one: Tom's relatives arrived and talked about themselves, again; Paul kept them away from me as much as possible, again; my brother dealt with the shopping, again; my mother and I prepared a meal, again, this time helped by Bea. And all the while, the phone and the doorbell kept up their seemingly synchronised alternate ringing...

By the evening, with Tom's relatives once again gone and my own mother and brother waved off with as much cheerfulness as I could muster, my voice had disappeared completely. Paul, Bea and I ate a hot, comforting meal on trays in front of the fire, making the most of our time together as they, too, would have to leave the next day. But not before Paul and I had completed a task which we both felt we had to do – the viewing of Tom's body. But that was for tomorrow; for that evening, I was simply grateful for Paul and Bea's company.

Paul felt very strongly that he actually wanted to see his father for one last time; perhaps to help him start along his own personal road to an acceptance that this terrible event had actually happened to our family. For me, though, it was simply a case of hoping to imprint on my mind a slightly less ghastly final image than the one which was currently lodged behind my eyelids, and seared into my brain. And so we went, Paul driving us in his car: I had gently discussed with him the possible effects of shock on seeing his father's body, but he was adamant.

The wait in the anteroom was almost unbearable, and I felt my heart rate rise and a sweat breaking out on my forehead. But I was in no danger of fainting, or of becoming hysterical. I neither cried nor gasped as I approached my husband's coffin; seeing his body was an expected shock. But I came away from that almost unbearably harrowing experience with, yes, certainly a very slightly less ghastly final image, although one which still left me shocked and shaken. Although the funeral directors had done an excellent job, of course, the body encased there wasn't my husband. Bearing in mind that he'd now been dead – by violence – for more than ten days, and his body had been subject to a full post-mortem, his appearance could not be described as peaceful, or 'asleep', or any of the other euphemisms designed to offer comfort, and maybe even a degree of hope. Speaking for myself, there could be no comfort, and any question of hope for the future was still too far distant to be even remotely relevant.

Paul and I walked back to his car through driving sleet, though the chill in the air was nothing compared to the chill which had seeped into our hearts and even, so it felt, into our bones. We returned home, trying to keep at bay the desolation which we were each feeling. My heart grieved more for my younger son than for myself during that bleak drive home. Paul had last seen his father in the warmth and fun of our Christmas celebration, just days previously, and now he had endured the self-imposed duty of seeing his father's body, the sight of that dead face imprinted indelibly on both our minds. Paul's driving was admirably calm and alert.

In our absence, Bea had prepared lunch. Time was now pressing, as Paul and Bea would have to leave that afternoon. As usual, though, our meal was interrupted by both the telephone and the doorbell. Still, we made the best possible use of the rapidly evaporating time. As I'd done with Mark, I waved them off with all the cheerfulness I could muster. But the closing of the front door behind their disappearing car sent a dull echo around the empty house, which suddenly seemed terribly large. Determinedly, I grabbed the dog lead, the dog, and my boots; a walk in the fields, followed by a cup of tea beside the fire, would need to be sufficient to dispel the gloom and to deal with any inclination to indulge myself in feelings of loneliness or self-pity.

The time had come for me to start learning to live alone.

Chapter 8: Shockwaves

My first night alone. Once I found myself alone for long enough to *be* really alone, that is, as the ripples from this dark pool of horror spread ever further outwards. With well-intentioned zeal to support me, the stream of visitors was continuing unabated, just as the stream of phone calls was continuing, equally unabated, and all oblivious to my barely-there voice, weak and croaking from simple overuse. More importantly, I was now reaching the point of utter exhaustion. And still they came, and still they phoned, just to make sure I was alright, not knowing how else to express their shock and concern. After all, this was new territory for everyone, not just for me. But despite the kindness and the care, it could be disconcerting at times, until I felt that I was being steadily engulfed by a tidal wave of well-meant but overwhelming sympathy.

Eight o'clock on that first evening, and the village, a totally streetlight-free zone, was quietly blanketed in its usual complete darkness. I sat on the sofa bed in my study, with my dog cuddled up beside me and the electric fire flickering, and answered emails. Just a few; then I would walk Misty, briefly, before going back to my study to concentrate on a book until it was time to flop thankfully into bed.

The doorbell rang, sudden and loud in the silent house; I ignored its insistent ringing and tried to soothe Misty's alarmed barking. Another ring; still I ignored it, despite Misty's increasingly agitated barks. The third ring was accompanied by a scuffling sound at the front door; Misty growled and I froze into stillness, my senses straining. And then a voice shouted through the letterbox. Misty, now barking frenetically and apparently determined to dismantle the letterbox and preferably the caller on the other side, leapt from the sofa and was off down the stairs like a greyhound out of the starting gate. Whoever it was, that bark said, would first have to get past Misty, the would-be Rottweiler in defence of her one remaining human.

"It's only me," called the voice. "I've come to make sure you're okay."

Another neighbour, then, this one wanting to tell me how she'd just returned home from her Christmas holiday and heard the awful news. With the most extreme reluctance I opened the door, contorting myself as I did so to hold onto my now snarling dog. The beam of my visitor's torch must surely have thrown my pale and wary face into even sharper relief, but in one swift movement she was through the door and enveloping me in a massive, emotional hug. Powerless to stop the flow of condolences, I felt forced by simple good manners to invite her into the sitting room, currently dark and abandoned. While switching on lamps, drawing curtains and acknowledging her concern, I could feel the plans I had made so carefully, bracing myself to get through this first evening in successful solitude, slipping away from me on that never-ending tide of well-meaning but wearying sympathy. By the time my visitor left, an hour or so later – and only then because the telephone kept ringing at approximately ten-minute intervals – my mind and senses were numb from sheer tiredness. But at least that meant sleep would come, heavy and, as it turned out, mercifully dreamless.

There was a sense of achievement on waking, that first morning alone, and realising that not only had I slept for several hours undisturbed, but that I'd been able to fall asleep relatively easily in the first place. In addition to learning to live alone in that suddenly vast-seeming house, I was of course fighting a nightly battle with the image of my husband's dead body, which came into full and ghastly focus as soon as I closed my eyes. Seeing him in his coffin had not, in fact, helped to dispel that earlier and horrifyingly stronger image.

But I had quickly developed my own way of dealing with that image: however tired I was on getting into bed, before trying to sleep I would read for an hour or so from one of a careful selection of favourite books. A lifelong bookworm, I had never been as heavily reliant on my books as in those first weeks, and indeed months, after such a massive shock as discovering my husband's suicide.

That first 24-hour period alone had given me a new mantra: I've done one day and one night alone, so now I can do another.

The days were filled with unrelenting activity: the usual arrangements to be made after any death, compounded in this case by the involvement of the police and the coroner. But the most terrifying facet of my new situation was my unfolding financial crisis which, as was becoming shockingly apparent, had been largely orchestrated by my husband. Not only had he emptied our current and savings accounts and stopped our credit cards, but he had apparently transferred the major part of our investments just before his death, leaving little or no record of his manoeuvrings. He had then either destroyed or effectively concealed both his 'home' and his 'office' laptops; either way, they were never found, despite a thorough search of the house, the gardens and the riverbank. Mark and Paul had even conducted their own dredging operation along the stretch of the river immediately beyond our garden. Watching that fruitless search turning up nothing except mud, I couldn't help thinking back to the enthusiasm with which Tom and I had realised our dream of living beside a river, blissfully unaware that our dream would soon be drowned in a nightmare.

Clearly Tom's mind must have been wildly mis-firing, like a crazily malfunctioning computer itself, during those final hours when he was somehow continuing to function physically despite cataclysmic mental collapse. Mercifully, though, he hadn't thought to destroy my own laptop. It had been in full view, there on the desk in my study upstairs. But perhaps, during those final hours alone, he simply didn't go upstairs…

My laptop's version gave only a limited view of our finances – Tom had apparently 'blocked' my view to some extent – but at least it was a start. Methodically, unflappably, my solicitor's assembled team of experts set to work to glean as much information as they could from my own computer, in the absence of Tom's.

Meanwhile, I finally had a date for the funeral, which couldn't be set until I had a death certificate. This wasn't the usual, definitive certificate stating the cause of death, but an 'interim' version purely to allow cremation, as the cause of death remained under investigation. I had seen the cause of death with my own horrified eyes, but the wheels of legality evidently needed to take their grinding course. Anyway, at least I had a date.

So now all the usual arrangements could be made, and the network of village facilities swung into smooth and concerted action, which in turn meant that the first flurry of shocked hyperactivity would now begin to subside. The church organist, together with his family, was particularly supportive and suggested suitable funeral music; I still felt completely unable even to begin thinking about such details for myself. Sitting by a blazing fire while he played me a selection of sensitively-chosen pieces, after a relaxed lunch at their house, I felt the warmth of assurance that I truly was not abandoned, and that somehow, eventually, my family and I would emerge from our nightmare. After another couple of days spent entirely on the phone, or so it seemed, I could feel that the arrangements were coming together, and therefore – just as importantly to me – I was starting to gain a measure of control; I was no longer totally paralysed by shock.

It was at this stage that my actual nightmares started in earnest, perhaps not surprisingly, as the anaesthetic of shock was beginning to wear off. They didn't recur every night, or cause me to wake screaming, but each nightmare was vivid enough to unsettle me. I would wake sweating and shivering, often horrified afresh by the pictures, and equally by the words, which my subconscious had released. But I was determined to look on it as just that: a release by the subconscious into the conscious mind. After all, I reassured myself, if the memory is the filing cabinet of the brain, then all those loose and disordered thoughts must first be brought out and viewed in the light, before the brain can decide where and how to file them away in an orderly fashion. I also used these alarms to make my first night-time excursions downstairs since living alone, making soothing hot drinks to help restore my mental equilibrium and comfort my physical reactions. And so my nocturnal alarums and excursions became another small victory; another tentative step on my intensely private road to overcoming the horror into which I had been so unexpectedly thrust.

A small but important victory came when I started to drive again, about two weeks after Tom's death. The local Police

Community Support Officer had popped in to reassure me about parking arrangements at the church, and the plans for keeping an eye on my house during the funeral. He took the opportunity of offering to put my car on the drive so that I could use it without needing to enter the garage: I wasn't ready for that, yet. But I was at least ready to drive (as the PCSO had evidently realised), so I accepted his offer gratefully. And as I subsequently drove myself home from my first solo appointment – at the funeral directors, a couple of miles away – I felt a real sense of achievement.

The next victory came first thing in the morning a few days later, when I had to scrape thick ice from my car to drive myself to a doctor's appointment. Pausing in mid-scrape, I decided this was a ridiculously unnecessary procedure, as I was the owner of a perfectly usable garage. So, on returning home in bright winter sunshine, I opened the garage door remotely and reversed my car in, as I had last done on that dreadful day. Opening the car door, I could not bring myself to turn round as I had done then. But I could, instead, walk purposefully out via the up-and-over door, to enter the house through the front door. Safely indoors, I was shaking with trauma, relief and, yes, pride. I'd done it: another small victory, but I now knew that I had set myself on the road to recovery and to independence. There would be setbacks on that road, naturally: in fact, two of them arrived that same evening, in unexpected and unpleasant tandem.

First to phone me with his complaints was the particular relative of Tom's who believed himself to be suffering so much more than myself. Indeed, anyone overhearing him would have received the distinct impression that my husband had committed suicide merely to inconvenience this relative. Not only had it played merry hell with his travel plans, apparently, but Tom had been in the process of 'advising' him in some financial capacity. More importantly he disapproved, in the strongest and loudest terms, of the arrangements I was making for the funeral. I listened to his complaints for a considerable time, while an ice-cold anger grew steadily inside me. Eventually I had to interrupt, simply to stem the flow, and so I informed this relative that I would not be changing any of the arrangements I had made, and I had no knowledge of any financial dealings in which my husband may have been involved. As the tirade seemed set to begin again, I ended the call, shaking with anger and contempt at his crass insensitivity.

My usual remedy for such trauma being a cup of tea, I had no sooner made it and settled down when the phone rang again. The caller display showed a number I didn't recognise, but that meant nothing, given the volume of calls I was receiving. I answered it, and a wheedling, South London-accented voice informed me that this was a relative of Tom's aunt who was in a care home. The caller, actually a relative of the aunt's late husband, informed me that Tom had been 'looking after' £18,500 of the aunt's money – her life savings, naturally – under a Power of Attorney. This man required immediate repayment of the money to himself on behalf of the aunt, together with the return of her wedding ring and other jewellery which Tom had, apparently, also been 'looking after'.

I listened in stunned silence. I had never heard of Tom holding a Power of Attorney, or of the £18,500: apart from the money my mother was lending me, I currently appeared to have barely £18.50 to my name, let alone £18,500. Pulling myself together, I interrupted this tirade, as I had interrupted the previous relative's tirade. Coldly, I informed this man that I knew nothing of the matter, and could only give him my solicitor's phone number. I then refused to enter into any further discussion, and ended the call.

I believe that evening was the closest I ever came to sheer panic. I paced the empty house, Misty at my heels, as I repeated yet another mantra: *Don't Panic*. But unlike Corporal Jones in Dad's Army, whose catchphrase that had originally been, this was no joke. And although I would not, *must* not, allow myself to panic, I was seriously unnerved. I was beginning to realise that I would have to fight for my own survival, now, and that realisation in itself seemed to give me the strength to bring the rising sense of panic under control.

Fortunately unable to see into the future, I told myself that surely my circumstances could not get any worse.

Chapter 9: Heart and soul

Meanwhile, though, the funeral arrangements were now all in place. The village inn, conveniently located and with its own car park, had the catering arrangements perfectly well organised; the church flower ladies were busy making two tall pedestal arrangements, beautifully restrained, in sombre purple against deepest green winter foliage, which were to stand on either side of the bier; the music and hymns were set and would bring a much-needed sense of peace to the service. I'd chosen a large but simple wreath of pure white early-spring blooms for the coffin; given the circumstances, there were to be no other flowers. Without needing to be asked, the PCSO had arranged to close the main road for the cortège.

Mark and Paul were each keen to give a short eulogy, and I decided to read Psalm 23, *The Lord is my Shepherd*, myself. I felt it might help my sons if I were to read immediately before they spoke, as a gesture of solidarity with them and, hopefully, giving them a few moments to steady themselves before this particular part of their ordeal. They both agreed readily. Their father had been their role model, and so to witness their agony, their shatteringly cruel disillusion, felt like an equally cruel, additional twist of the knife lodged in my own heart. I felt yet again that I would have given anything, endured any pain myself, if I could only have saved my sons from such torment.

While the funeral arrangements were being finalised, work continued on the financial crisis and the mass of unfinished business which Tom had left behind. The documents which my solicitor had removed initially from Tom's home office had included a list of account numbers in Tom's own handwriting, running to *twelve pages* of A4 paper. And in those twelve pages lay a substantial part of the answer to the mystery of the missing funds. Apparently as part of his ever-increasing mental overload, Tom had been constructing his own private financial merry-go-round, endlessly switching money amongst innumerable online accounts in his sole name but, in the absence of his computer, leaving no record of his machinations. And then, finally, on the day of his death Tom had transferred the balance of our joint accounts out of my reach, too.

Viewed along with the eleven mobile phones and the mountains of personal and work-related documents, I began to realise that the extent of this overload was far greater than I had ever imagined, and could easily be a physical symptom of Tom's unrecognised mental illness. I had no idea of how long that illness had been developing, of course, but it was beginning to seem likely that there was a predisposition to such problems within his own character.

As I had silently howled into the empty night, in my initial stunned shock and disbelief, the Tom I knew would *never* have inflicted this agony on his family. He was always motivated by kindness and care for others, and would never say 'no' to anyone in need of help. But I returned continually to the fact that he never took time for himself; that he was hyperactive, a workaholic and a perfectionist. Adding up all that he did for the family and for other people, plus his responsibility at work, the inescapable conclusion, in the stark and bleak light of hindsight, seemed to be that his own goodness had been his downfall. My husband was an intensely private person who never discussed his feelings, and believed totally in his own self-reliance, with the result that when he reached the stage of complete mental overload he couldn't, or wouldn't, cry out for help. So I tried to hold fast to the belief that the man who did inflict this agony on his family was not the same person as my kind, caring husband. Silent and unnoticed, the real Tom must already have died.

The day before the funeral; it would have been Tom's 57th birthday. My sons, my mother and my brother were all once again with me. As always, nowadays, I was awake very early, and having made tea, I sat up in bed watching dawn break over the wintry landscape. Snow was now lying, treacherous in places, but I knew that wouldn't stop Tom's family and, as expected, by mid-morning the house seemed to be swarming with people.

The particular relative had been the first to arrive, of course, loudly demanding to know where he could find my mother-in-law's jewellery, as he'd decided it must be in my house somewhere. Had I been able to lay my hands on it, I would probably have thrown it at him. But at least I persuaded him to take away the dozen or more removal boxes containing the bedridden aunt's possessions. All except *her* jewellery, apparently; the particular relative declared that he would make a thorough search of my house for both the missing sets of jewellery. I informed him, curtly, that he would not.

By the time they had all left, several hours later, I could think of nothing except trying to ensure some sort of peaceful interlude for my family and myself. For the first time, that evening I allowed the phone to go unanswered and the emails unread.

What can be said about any one funeral, which has not been said about a million other funerals? It passed, with the calm dignity and decorous sadness befitting our particular circumstances, and yet with its own muted intensity which seemed to permeate every moment of that unreal day. I had closed all the curtains at the front of the house, in the old-fashioned gesture of mourning, before the hearse approached along the village street. Tom's two immediate relatives had declined to travel with my family and myself in the limousine which would follow the hearse, preferring to accompany the coffin itself. I found that gesture rather moving: as brusque and even bullying as some of Tom's relatives may be towards me, they must have been feeling their own intense grief at his death, and would have to deal with it in their own way.

And so, with my sons, my mother and my brother, I took my place for a journey which, though actually very short, had a sense of timelessness. The main road appeared to be suspended in an unnatural and almost eerie mid-morning silence, as the clergy walked ahead of the cortège, their formal black outer cloaks billowing in the breeze like enormous dark wings. I refused to allow my imagination to see any symbolism in that, and simply gazed unseeing out of the silent limousine. There was no one lining that short route from the house to the parish church: the entire population of the village seemed to be there already, awaiting our arrival in a still incredulous silence.

Preparing to follow my husband's coffin into the church, I linked arms with my sons, who had taken their places one on each side of me. I checked again that my mother was coping, in the bitter weather and the even more bitter circumstances. Silent and resolute on the arm of my brother, she stood ready to follow us. So too did my husband's cousin-cum-best-friend, walking alongside the particular relative who had not, I now noticed with distaste, seen fit to remove his gaudy diamanté ear studs for the occasion.

But the crass incongruity of his appearance paled into insignificance, along with everything and everyone else, as my immediate family and I braced ourselves for our own soul-wrenching farewell.

There was a sense of unreality as we entered the packed church: three weeks after this most unnatural death, we were still too shocked to do anything other than function on auto-pilot. So, as I prepared to say my final goodbye to my life's partner, I felt only unutterable sadness: the deepest emotion and the rawest grief would, for me at least, need to be faced and dealt with privately. In my family, we still feel that grief is a private emotion rather than a public spectacle, and so we did not weep. On the contrary, I sat, and stood, and sang, as if I found myself unexpectedly in the middle of some sort of slow-motion and nightmarish stage set. Self-contained, determined, and ice-cold right to my heart, I went through the motions of this most solemn and almost unbearably final rite, all the while continuing to struggle with disbelief that our marriage, and our wider family life, could have ended like this.

Mark and Paul each spoke with a calm authority which belied their years, and a deep emotion which proved their love for their father, with no need for histrionics. And as I read the well-remembered psalm, I concentrated purely on the delivery of each phrase, and on speaking to each person present as my eyes swept the congregation. I felt I owed that much to Tom; reading those timeless, wise words in an effort simply to soothe, since there could be no explaining the inexplicable, for his sake as much as for that of myself and our sons.

The hardest moment for all my family came at the crematorium, where Mark and Paul took their places as pall-bearers, in their final act of service and devotion to their father. (Places had likewise been offered to the particular relative and the cousin, neither of whom, apparently, felt equal to the task.) Resolute and dignified, but with a pain behind their eyes which ripped into my heart even as it swelled with pride, my sons continued to bear their searing pain and disbelief in public, with exemplary and unflinching courage. And then, as the curtains gently closed and the coffin was gone, I felt the suppressed tension shuddering through their six-foot tall frames, standing so closely one on either side of me, as the loss of their father, and under such circumstances, became agonisingly final.

Meeting and greeting family and friends after the cremation had that now horribly familiar air of unreality. The inn had laid on an excellent buffet, though of course I personally ate nothing. Despite being constantly busy – making sure I talked to each person, checking everyone was well supplied with platefuls of food, etc. – occasionally the remains of my heart would lurch, as my memory involuntarily called up other buffets at other family gatherings, such as my sons' christenings. Then I would feel a fresh stab of pain because Tom was not by my side and never would be again, through his own choice.

But I was able to draw immense comfort from being amongst people so dear to me, including school friends who'd known me since we were eleven years old. Their love for me, and their horror at my circumstances, were palpable in equal measure. A succession of people held me close, that day; tightly, wordlessly and with the deepest pools of sympathy in their eyes, as though their hearts would break alongside my own.

And then the funeral was over at last, and the relatives, even the particular one and his immediate family, were finally gone. Trauma on such a massive scale as that caused by suicide, and in my case by having discovered my husband's body myself, had blanked out everything but the unfolding practical demands of my own and my family's situation. Even the ability to shed tears in private had been deeply buried beneath the sheer enormity of the blow from which we were still reeling. By now my mind had been able to accept the practicalities of my family's grotesquely altered circumstances, and yet it still seemed inconceivable, in those few quiet moments when I could pause from almost ceaseless activity and try to digest that hateful word *suicide*, that this had happened to us. Actually and indisputably to us, not to some other family about whom we could simply read in a newspaper, shake our heads in the uncomprehending sympathy of common humanity, and then turn the page to go on with our ordinary and ordered lives.

I had hoped that in the aftermath of the funeral, my immediate family and I might have peace enough to begin the process, long-delayed by the very deepest shock and by the machinations of the judiciary, known as 'normal' grieving. But at that stage I had no idea of all the additional pain which was yet to come.

Chapter 10: A detective calls

The following day passed in a haze of exhaustion; mental, physical and emotional. And then the next drama burst upon us.

Mark and Paul were relieving their feelings by chopping up the discarded Christmas tree in the garden, using a noisy old chainsaw they'd unearthed from the shed. My mother was sitting at my desk upstairs, working on her correspondence; informing the more distant and far-flung relatives, and her own friends, of what had happened in our family. Angela and I had gone out together, as we each had an appointment with the local building society manager to discuss our individual financial positions. Angela's appointment was finished, and I was beginning to feel cautiously optimistic for my longer-term future, as my own interview progressed, when Angela received a call on her mobile phone from her daughter: Angela's house had just been broken into.

Apparently the intruders had crept through the rear garden and kicked down the back door under cover of the chainsaw's noise, while Mark and Paul were just yards away on the other side of the screening hedge. The arrival of Angela's daughter on the drive had alerted the burglars, who were just then busily ransacking Angela's bedroom, situated at the front of the house. While Angela's daughter was unloading her car in the front garden, the burglars had time to escape the way they had come, through the rear garden. Walking round to enter the house via the back door, Angela's daughter saw the swinging, damaged door, and screamed. Mark and Paul, who had just that moment switched off the chain saw, scaled both hedge and fence with an ease born of real alarm, and tore into the house. It was probably fortunate for all concerned that the burglars had already escaped, since Paul, a judo black belt, would have taken instinctive and drastic revenge, not only for the burglars' intrusion, but also for the events devastating our own lives. There would quite possibly have been bits of burglar all over the place, and I had enough trouble on my own hands already, without a return to the local police station, this time to bail out my son! In any case, the circumstances would have done nothing for my reputation with the local constabulary, which would hardly have helped, perhaps, in my eventual encounter with the coroner.

Meanwhile, though, the immediate priority was Angela. Arriving home and taking her straight to my house as the police were still busy in hers, I quickly told my mother what had happened, while making hot drinks. Angela's daughter arrived bringing with her Angela's elderly dog, who had slept peacefully throughout the burglary and was unharmed, to everyone's intense relief. Misty rather touchingly took charge of her friend, and the two dogs settled companionably side by side on a large cushion in the French windows, nose to nose, looking as though they were quietly discussing the morning's dramatic events.

I was about to serve hot soup, along with savouries left over from the funeral, when the police arrived to talk to Angela. Offering what comfort I could seemed a pitifully small return for all that she had done for me on the evening of Tom's death, but it made me feel useful, and therefore just a little better.

But my mind kept returning to the earlier part of that ghastly day; to the morning, when Tom had examined the broken lock on Angela's back door, and promised to come round that same afternoon to fix it.

Eventually, a couple of days after the burglary, I finally found myself alone once more, in the uneasy calm which seems to follow any funeral. They'd all gone; Mark, with Clare and her family, back to their own home in the north, heartbroken at leaving me and aghast at the extent and implications of the agony which had engulfed us. Paul back to the southwest, to work out his misery physically, on the farm and in the sea. My mother, so tiny and frail but of such mighty stature when and how it matters, taken home by my brother. The friends and relations, quite rightly and properly, back to their own lives; kindly making endless phone calls, so that my throat still hurt by the end of each day, and sending me an endless stream of emails.

But all these demonstrations of continuing concern and solicitous efforts to keep in touch meant that I could never feel abandoned, even at those times when it didn't feel too comfortable to be alone in that sizeable house, after everything which had happened there. I told myself I'd lived alone for a week before the funeral; so now I could manage another week, and then another...

Those weeks were busy, naturally. In between appointments, I began to turn out firstly Tom's late parents' possessions, of which there were still more than a dozen large, removal company boxfuls. My mother-in-law had died almost twenty years previously, but there lay all her most prized possessions, wrapped in old newspapers; all, that is, except her jewellery. With his parents' possessions as with everything else, Tom had been unable to let go, although I had to assume by now that for reasons of his own he must have hidden or destroyed his mother's jewellery since, like his own laptops, no trace of it was ever found.

In the wake of the burglary, a policewoman came to see Angela and myself about home security. It turned out during the initial conversation that she had also been a bereavement counsellor, so when my turn came, she and I just sat on my sofa and talked, over coffee. She was a superb counsellor, maybe even better for being, in this case, unintended and informal; unlike the young lady I had seen a few days previously at the doctor's surgery, who was a 'mental health expert'.

No older than my son Paul, this young lady was rather nervous, and had the air of a student who has inadvertently mislaid her tutor. Her appearance was exactly as might be expected: jet-black dyed hair, a flimsy black-and-white short tunic and thick black tights ending in chunky black boots, the overall effect being that she'd dashed out of the house in such a hurry that she'd forgotten to put on her skirt. Still, she'd obviously read the textbook, as she had her list of standard questions ready, plus my 'case notes'. These contained full details of my husband's death, and stated my occupation quite clearly as 'freelance writer'. Despite having this information to hand, her standard but almost unbearably crass questions – delivered in a nasal monotone – included such gems as:

did I have any thoughts of self-harm or suicide;
had I ever thought of trying to write things
down or keep a diary;
did I understand how to structure my day; and

did I realise that I mustn't give in to the temptation to watch television all day.

On being informed that I don't watch television, she looked startled, thought for a moment, and then handed me a booklet to accompany a TV programme especially for widows.

For me, at least, the bereavement counselling service had failed utterly, since it left me with the feeling that I was simply a case number, to be dealt with by ticking the necessary boxes on a form, which would then be assessed according to a set of fixed criteria. From the standard questions which I was asked, the priority seemed to be simply to ensure that I fitted into a convenient category and, most importantly perhaps, that I would not cause further inconvenience to the system, by committing suicide in my turn!

The only relief this particular young counsellor had been capable of offering me was totally unintentional, by way of amusement at her total lack of experience, empathy or understanding. Unfortunately, her sole success on this occasion had been to put me off the whole concept of counselling as a source of comfort or release, or of making at least some sense of what had gone so catastrophically wrong in Tom's mind, distorting his view of the world and his place in it, and warping his love for me out of all recognition. That was really the subject I had wanted to discuss with a counsellor, because I had hoped that some attempt at understanding his complete mental meltdown would in turn have helped to calm the turmoil in my own mind. Perhaps it might also have helped me to deal with the anger which was later to take hold of me, growing in intensity until it consumed my love for my late husband in a raging furnace of fury and misery. But I would need to look elsewhere for help in dealing with that – to my family and friends – and in the meantime I decided I would derive far greater comfort from a walk in the countryside with my dog, than from any further counselling sessions.

Far more seriously, I then received a phone call from the coroner's office, to tell me the date on which a detective constable would be sent to take the formal statement from me. I resisted the temptation to take refuge in flippancy and ask why I didn't merit a detective inspector, at the very least.

The young DC duly arrived; at least he was dressed properly, and had a certain air of experienced authority, unlike the young counsellor. Again I was required to go through all the details of finding my husband's body, which included the detective's accompanying me to the garage. That proved to be an acutely painful experience, as officialdom intruded on the scene of the most intense personal grief, shock and horror. Forcing myself to remain calm, I pointed out exactly how and where I had reversed my car into the garage, to demonstrate – in answer to his question – why I did not see the body until I had got out of the car and turned round to go indoors. The DC made copious notes but no comment. Back in the house once more, I was then required to answer a stream of extremely personal questions, on the grounds that:

"The coroner will want answers."

I replied that perhaps the coroner should learn the lesson that in life we do not always get what we might want...

Again I was pressed hard over the undated letter which had been taken from my husband's briefcase, and again I stated clearly and unequivocally the true circumstances under which that letter had been written, in the wake of a marital row about the family finances some three years earlier. Again, however, it was apparent that I was not believed; the authorities were immovable in their belief that I was lying, and that the row actually took place shortly before Tom's death. A chill realisation began to dawn on me that this hateful letter really was going to be used at the inquest, in an attempt to implicate me as a cause of my husband's suicide.

The interview lasted two hours, at the end of which, although I had been unsettled by the detective's evident disbelief over the undated letter, I mercifully had no indication of the persistence with which the coroner would subsequently use that letter against me at the inquest. Meanwhile, though, as the DC put away his pen and filed away my signed statement, he praised me for my stoicism; apparently it is most unusual, nowadays, to deal with a woman who doesn't break down and cry.

In fact, I have since discovered that modern psychotherapists extol the virtues of weeping, the recently-expounded expert view being that to cry in public 'shows you can express yourself'. And so, unrealised by me at the time of that interview, my determined self-restraint could actually count against me, since modern British society seems to find self-control unusual and even unnatural. Instead, personal grief is apparently expected to be put on unrestrained display, whether at a funeral, in a police interview – or in a coroner's court.

Chapter 11: Web of intrigue

After the funeral, the burglary and the counsellor, plus the detective constable of my very own (my private detective, as it were), came a return to the more usual practicalities of death, alongside the less usual aftermath caused by the bleak fact of suicide. The loss of Tom's computer continued to prey on my mind. Knowing that he had emptied our accounts and transferred most of our savings out of my immediate reach, including the transfer of some funds abroad, I now feared for whatever else he may have done without my knowledge, and whatever other steps he may have taken against me. Meanwhile, as expected, it was confirmed that the life assurance policy which Tom had taken out years ago, with me as the beneficiary, would not pay out as his death was by suicide. So much for life assurance with all its prettily 'reassuring' platitudes, I thought bitterly, as my sense of financial desolation continued to grow.

Using my own laptop's limited view of our financial affairs, together with the vast quantity of documents removed from Tom's home office, my solicitor's team were obtaining a clearer picture of his financial dealings, most of which had been conducted online. Now that we had a death certificate, albeit only an interim version, the various financial institutions would be obliged to provide full details of all his assets and – terrible thought – any liabilities. Gradually, painstakingly, the financial entanglements would be unravelled, but in the meantime they were costing me additional sleepless nights, and additional legal fees, of course.

A necessary part of the whole process was for the solicitor in charge of Tom's estate to check and photocopy our original marriage certificate. This lady became an important part of my personal support network, and we would meet regularly. During one of these meetings, at Riverside, I left her with a cup of coffee and a stack of documents, while I went to fetch the certificate from my own file of personal papers. This was where the marriage certificate had been kept, along with my birth certificate, throughout the thirty-one years of our marriage.

It was gone.

I returned to the sitting room, shaking with disbelief, and sat down while the solicitor went to the kitchen to make us yet more coffee. Although she told me not to worry, as an official copy certificate could easily be obtained (though at a cost), I could see that she was almost as shocked by this latest twist as I was. Surely there could no longer be any doubt: during the weeks since his death, it had become increasingly and agonisingly clear that my husband had laid his plans with extreme care and cold-blooded determination. Not only for his actual suicide, but even for some sort of war of attrition against me, which he'd apparently intended to wage from beyond the noose. That night, I was once again ill with some sort of stomach bug, no doubt simply as a reaction to the layer upon layer of shock, coupled with sheer mental anguish.

Far worse than any type of stomach bug, though, was my particular type of corporate bug, which by this stage was reaching epidemic proportions. My husband's employers (of many years' standing) had been shuffling their collective feet for some time over confirming whether I would be entitled to the full widow's proportion of his occupational pension. Meanwhile his own department was shuffling its feet in equally painful indecision, over collecting the vast quantity of confidential business papers still in Tom's study, together with the total of eleven mobile phones, three of which I'd found in his briefcase and the rest in various drawers and files in his study.

Added to all that, I had still received no response to the question of when his business landline at home would be disconnected. Distressingly for me, this phone was still receiving calls from business contacts who had evidently not yet heard the news of Tom's death.

But the crunch came on receipt of a letter from his employers' marketing department, almost three months after Tom's death, addressed to 'Mr Tom RobertsHomeworker'. This letter informed 'Dear Tom' that 'since you left us, further charges have been incurred on your homeworker account: please phone...' etc. I'd intended to put a final warning shot across the company's bows in any case, but that letter made me decide to launch a full-scale attack. The letter to the Chief Executive was the most important, of course, but the emails and phone calls yielded results, too. I found myself needing to upbraid a senior marketing executive for attempting to interrupt and fob me off with jargon; the reticent-and-retiring pensions manager was reduced almost to tears; Tom's boss, when his turn came, exhibited a slight stammer at the start of our conversation, but a far worse one by the end...

Within a few days, the eleven mobile phones and the confidential papers had been collected by courier, the landline had been switched off, the Head of Marketing had sent a letter of grovelling apology (correctly addressed to me), and my entitlement to a full widow's pension had been confirmed. Most intriguing of all, though, was a 'goodwill' payment made to me by the company, apparently separate from my pension entitlement. This payment was made without comment, but presumably as a gesture of remorse for the catalogue of mismanagement in the company's dealings with me since Tom's death. But it still came as a complete surprise to me, and felt strangely unsettling, because my motive in taking on the Chief Executive and his assorted minions had certainly not been mercenary. The 'RobertsHomeworker' letter had been an exceptionally crass error, which I was simply determined to prevent the company repeating in its treatment of any other widow in future. I felt very strongly that not everyone in my situation would feel able to laugh at such absurdity, as I had done once my initial anger had subsided. A desperately shocked, vulnerable and possibly lonely widow could conceivably be pushed into serious ill-health – perhaps even depression – on receiving such an appallingly insensitive communication. But the payment struck me as amounting to a tacit apology, and so I felt vindicated.

There had been absolutely no suggestion of any particular aspect of his work having been a cause of Tom's suicide. However, both the workload and the stress level had clearly been intense. When viewed in conjunction with the excessive quantity of business documents kept at home, and the eleven mobile phones, it all implied total overload.

How much of that overload was due to actual pressure of work, and how much to Tom's own perception of his position as a senior employee, given that he was a passionate workaholic, remained a matter of pure conjecture. But presumably that particular question had in any case given the company's top-level management a nasty moment; after all, any accusation of blame for the suicide of a senior employee – and one who apparently had everything to live for – would hardly constitute good publicity for the company, however unfounded or even hysterical such an accusation might prove to be.

Meanwhile the company's 'Bereavement Team' had of course dismally failed to take any of the steps necessary on an employee's death, such as arranging to switch off the business phone and voicemail, or preventing the 'RobertsHomeworker' letter, far less sending me any word or gesture of condolence. Not to be outdone in the apology stakes, they now sent me their contribution. This was not a bouquet of flowers, as might perhaps have been appropriate, but a card containing the words:

"Sorry, Lucy. Treat yourself to something nice."

The card was accompanied by: a £20 department store voucher! I decided it would be more constructive to feel amused than insulted.

At this point in the proceedings I began to feel distinctly better: I was starting to learn that there's nothing like a good scrap to pep up an ailing widow! More seriously, I fervently hoped I'd taught the Chief Executive and his sidekicks that they try to mess with a widow, merry or otherwise, at their collective peril.

While my legal team were all busy searching the web and elsewhere for the missing investments, a previously unknown and distinctly dodgy-sounding investment was busy crawling out of the woodwork all by itself. Or rather, out of the brickwork, since it involved me, to my intense surprise, as the joint owner with my husband of a property somewhere in Hertfordshire. Unfortunately, this turned out to be almost valueless. Completely unknown to me at the time, Tom had made a purchase through a land investment company which was now in liquidation. But when I first came upon the Land Registry papers tucked away in

Tom's study, my stomach lurched: did I have a house on this piece of land and, if so, was it tenanted? Upkeep, repairs, liabilities... All these potential disaster areas began to parade through my imagination, each waving a large bill at me. But it turned out to be quite simply a tiny plot of unused land.

Apparently these so-called investment companies buy a parcel of cheap, undesirable brownfield-site land within reach of, perhaps, a major motorway or an existing urban centre. They then sub-divide it into tiny individual plots, which are legitimately registered at the Land Registry and marketed as a 'prime residential development opportunity'. No development is ever intended, of course. The company goes into liquidation after its directors have taken the profit from the multiple plot sales, and the 'investors' are left with almost worthless pieces of land. The documents in his study revealed that Tom had learned of the company's liquidation and the inevitable failure of his 'investment', which would have dealt yet another blow to his pride and sense of self-worth.

My solicitor set about selling the land at auction: it raised barely a thousand pounds, almost half of which was then accounted for by legal and auctioneer's fees. There was also a pre-existing covenant which obliged me to pay 50% of the sale proceeds to the vendor who originally sold the land to the development company. So I was left with just a few pounds. I could hardly feel cheated, since I hadn't even known of its existence, but I was disappointed that my particular plot hadn't turned out to be a more substantial chunk of Hertfordshire: I'd rather like to have been the self-styled Queen of Herts.

Meanwhile, the bedridden aunt's relative continued to press for the return of the missing £18,500, and now so, too, did Tom's own particular relative. These two solicitous gentlemen each claimed to have taken out a Power of Attorney, giving him the right to handle the aunt's funds in place of Tom. When my solicitor requested a copy of each of these much-vaunted documents, a certain amount of telephonic bluster ensued before, finally and perhaps not altogether surprisingly, it transpired that neither of these dutiful relatives held a Power of Attorney at all. But of greater concern to me, and far more shockingly, *neither did Tom.* No such document was ever found amongst his massive quantity of papers, nor was it in the aunt's possession, nor had it ever been legally registered.

Evidently, then, Tom had been 'looking after' his aunt's money on a purely informal basis, but there was no separate account; in fact, at that stage there was no trace of the money at all. Investigations continued, sometimes seeming agonisingly slow in the absence of Tom's computer, his passwords and other data, but eventually the aunt's life savings were traced. Tom had simply placed the money into some form of online investment portfolio, but under his own name which, legally speaking, he should not have done.

By this stage, our own savings and Tom's sole investments were gradually being tracked down and recovered, too, though the whole process took many months. But at least I now knew that most, if not quite all, of our savings were recoverable. So the financial crisis which had initially seemed overwhelming, receded at last, to my equally overwhelming relief.

Although I was still too deeply shocked – and probably traumatised – to take in the full implications of my husband's apparently premeditated actions against me, I was nevertheless starting to feel the first stirrings of anger against the man who could do this to his own wife. That rising tide of anger was beginning to swamp the kinder, gentler conviction that Tom must already have been beyond all reason when he planned his very own and virtually worldwide web of intrigue. And my anger very soon led to something else: an implacable determination not to let him beat me. However unjustly, my situation was beginning to feel less like a bereavement and more like a particularly acrimonious divorce. I would fight, now, to regain my full financial security, my reputation as being uninvolved in his suicide, and (eventually) my peace of mind. But in order to come through this agonising process and emerge on the other side with my own sanity intact, I was going to need strength, determination – and a sense of humour.

And so I felt the 'die' had been cast.

Chapter 12: Is there anyone there?

Quite separately from the corporate tussle over switching off Tom's 'homeworker' business line, our domestic phone and broadband provider needed to transfer the personal account into my sole name, of course. Simple, I thought, in my technologically unwashed innocence. I explained the situation by phone to the relevant adviser, and was asked for the principal account holder's security password. Naturally enough, I was unable to supply this or any other security details, the principal account holder being my late husband. Unfortunately this meant that I had failed the security clearance test. The only way to proceed, the adviser assured me perfectly seriously, was for her to talk to my husband personally. I repeated, unequivocally, that my husband was deceased. The adviser repeated, just as unequivocally, that the only way to 'progress this issue' was by direct contact with the principal account holder. In whatever state of being, apparently, that account holder should happen to be.

Now, I know that telephony can achieve miraculous things nowadays, but surely not *that* miraculous? Out of pure devilment, as it were, I suggested that when the adviser had set up the necessary séance, perhaps she would let me know, as there were a few things I'd rather like to say to my deceased husband, myself... As expected, this suggestion was greeted with an emphatically dead silence. The problem being, presumably, that holding a séance wasn't an option on the adviser's computer screen, and therefore she was unable to comment, or to offer any alternative solution to the computer's insistence that she must speak to the deceased, *please*.

We had reached deadlock, in a manner of speaking. Or rather, in a manner of not speaking. But following receipt of the stiffly-worded letter which I then felt obliged to send, the company did its very best to be helpful. Apparently the technological department could not find a way to remove my late husband's name as principal account holder, and substitute my own name. There was no way to reset the details so that bills, etc., would be sent in my name and I would be able to use the online account with my own security data. The entire setup would need to be scrapped, on production of the death certificate; uninstalled and then reinstalled as a completely different customer, with all the attendant irritations and delays. Such is the progress of technology!

While the telephone company didn't know how to speak to me because they needed to speak to the deceased, there were others who didn't know how to speak to me simply because of my change in circumstance, and the horrific event which had brought that change about. At those times I found myself at pains to put the other person at ease, which in turn made the situation much more relaxed for me, and therefore, hopefully, for the other person concerned.

One memorable example was my visit to the dentist, about three months after Tom's death. Usually it's the patient who's nervous of the dentist, but in my case, it was the dentist who was nervous of the patient! Our dentist hadn't seen me since the previous autumn, but she'd seen Tom just a couple of weeks before he died, and I'd had to phone the dental surgery to cancel his next appointment. So the dentist was fully aware of the circumstances, and now she came out to the waiting room herself, to conduct me gently and courteously into the surgery, with apprehension written all over her face and tension in all her movements.

It felt very strange to find myself in the position of putting a dentist at her ease, but I smiled and thanked her sincerely for her condolences, determined to show that it was business as usual as far as I was concerned. Everything was fine from then on, as the dentist visibly relaxed, and consequently my confidence in my ability to handle my circumstances rose considerably.

Not all situations were as easy to handle as that one had been, naturally, and not all the people involved were as considerate. It was now three months since Tom had died, and Saturday afternoons were still my least favourite time of the week. So I would make sure I had something to look forward to; a Saturday treat, however minor. It might be starting to read a new book, or something as simple as an individual homemade cake from the village shop, to enjoy with a cup of tea while sitting beside the fire in my safe, enclosing study.

I was about to enjoy just such a cake and cup of tea by the fire, one cold and dreary Saturday afternoon at the end of March, when the doorbell rang. I opened the door rather tentatively, not having been expecting anyone; neither had Misty, who as usual was barking at the mere idea. To my surprise, on the doorstep stood a man in his sixties and in full motorbike gear, clutching his helmet. Shuffling slightly from foot to foot, he enquired, politely enough, whether Tom was at home. I, in turn, enquired who he was, keeping my face as impassive as I could. He then introduced himself as the secretary of the motorbike club to which Tom had belonged and for which he had been running a website. Apparently various club members had been trying to contact Tom, both by phone and by email with, of course, no response. The club's committee had become so concerned at his silence that they had despatched their nearest member – a despatch rider, as it were – to find out what was wrong. My doorstep caller having provided sufficient information to remove any remaining doubts as to his identity, I felt safe in inviting him into the hall (I had by now learned to be extremely cautious, as a woman on my own). But I did keep this particular encounter as brief as possible, feeling totally unequal to discussing my husband's part in a motorbike club, or dealing with anything more than this man's own shocked and mumbled condolences. Having listened with courteous disinterest to his assurance that a suitable eulogy would appear in the next edition of the club's magazine, and responded appropriately, I politely but firmly brought our interview to a close.

At the time of his death, Tom didn't actually own a motorbike but a Lotus sports car, which he had intended to sell in the spring and return to motorbikes, his first love. He'd proudly assured me that the Lotus was very valuable, having been lovingly cared for. So our double garage, in which I had parked my car so blithely in the moments before discovering his body, also contained Tom's Lotus, while his everyday car was kept on a hard-standing area adjacent to the drive. My solicitor had offered to arrange for the sale of both cars, and was keen to have them removed for me as soon as possible in the aftermath of Tom's death.

The everyday car having been sold fairly easily, the solicitor's usual contact in the motor trade then struggled to find a buyer for the Lotus. A specialist inspection had revealed trouble with, amongst other things, a blown head gasket, while the engine was apparently not firing on all cylinders (I wasn't feeling too wonderful myself at that point, either). So the Lotus, of which my solicitor and I had previously had such expectations, finally raised a little over half the figure we'd hoped for, and presumably significantly less than Tom himself would have expected.

Anyway, the day finally came for its removal; a noisy low-loader arrived, and a rather brash man in a gaudy jacket strode down my drive, where he duly presented his card and driving licence for my inspection, as specified by my solicitor. I opened the garage. He walked slowly all around the Lotus, shaking his head and muttering; he peered into the interior; he opened the bonnet and then the car's miniscule boot. Although safe in the knowledge that my solicitor had already received the agreed price, I stiffened: was he about to try to re-negotiate? My solicitor had told me simply to check his identity documents and hand over the keys. Re-closing the boot with a degree of force which I felt was unnecessary, he announced that one or two 'extra parts' were missing:

"So I'll just have a scout around your garage for them."

Holding my mobile phone so that it was clearly visible and ready for immediate use, I informed this man that he would not 'scout around' my garage for missing parts or indeed for anything else, that the deal had already been concluded, and that he had my permission to take the car away. Right now. I didn't honestly believe that he posed any real threat either to myself or to my property, but I was extremely relieved to hear that mis-firing engine roaring up the steep drive for the last time, to close the garage and go indoors, and then, some minutes later, to see the sports car finally loaded onto the waiting truck and taken away. I was beginning to feel that I'd had more than enough of dealing with my late husband's possessions.

In addition to his physical possessions and financial dealings, there remained another matter concerning my husband which would need to be dealt with, this time in my own right: the question of his – our – surname. After the nightmarish ending of our 31-year marriage, the feeling had begun to grow steadily that I would need to revert to my maiden name, as part of my own personal recovery process. This re-adoption of my own surname would be no mere negative or retaliatory gesture against the memory of my late husband, but rather an affirmation of my own individual identity, as I prepared out of pure necessity to turn to the next chapter of my life. I wanted to assert to everyone who knew me, as well as to myself, that I could and did accept what had happened, that my marriage was over, and that I was ready to begin the painful process of laying it to rest. Only then would I be able to go on to start building a new life for myself from the wreckage of my marriage, as an independent single woman for the first time in my life.

The initial step was to put the idea to each of my sons, naturally. I was slightly nervous about telling them of my intentions, as I dreaded offending them, or wounding them further with the knowledge that I preferred to be known by a different surname from theirs. They each had enough pain to bear already. To my intense relief, both Mark and Paul immediately accepted and fully understood my reasons, and weren't in the least offended. Mark had recently become engaged to Clare, who had demonstrated both her deep love for him and her strength of character, in the support she gave Mark as he struggled to cope with the profound shock of his father's suicide. Once I was sure of both my sons' support, I discussed my intention with Clare, as Mark's fiancée. She and I easily agreed that in relinquishing the title of Mrs Roberts for myself, I would in effect be handing it on to her, as I would have finished with it and she was looking forward to taking it over. So that in this ending there would also be a beginning, and that struck us both as being entirely fitting.

Nothing could be done until after the investigation into my husband's death had been completed and a full death certificate issued, of course, but I expected the legal process for reverting to my maiden name to be straightforward. After all, I was only trying to take back the legal identity which had been mine in the first place. I assumed that this would involve simply the

79

production of our marriage certificate and my husband's death certificate, to prove that the marriage had taken place and was now legally ended by the death of one partner.

I couldn't have been more wrong. I would be required to go through the entire deed poll process, involving the drawing up of a full Change of Name Deed by my solicitors, with attendant documentation, certified copies and, of course, expense. But it still felt absolutely right. Which was fortunate, as the whole process took several months, and was further delayed by the many complications in winding up Tom's estate, probate having been granted to Mrs Lucy Roberts. My solicitor had warned me to stand by for complete chaos, which is precisely what ensued. I duly handed over my passport and driving licence, which had to be amended first and would, in any case, take several weeks. This would make me a sort of non-person, temporarily at least, which was a very odd feeling: if I should be asked to prove my identity formally, I would not be able to do so, or in any case not without assistance from my solicitor.

But at least the delay should give enough time for my internet service provider, still recovering from the 'principal account holder' fiasco, to work out how to deal with this latest change. Meanwhile the whole question of how to organise my name changeover would provide an alternative diversion for my thoughts, as I faced the next trauma which was now looming large on my horizon: the inquest into my husband's death.

Chapter 13: In quest of answers

"The coroner will want answers."

So the detective constable had warned me ominously, back in January. Now, on May Day – the following day would have been our thirty-second wedding anniversary – I was about to bear witness, literally, to the coroner's efforts to obtain not just any answers, but the answers he wanted. Perhaps in my case it wasn't so much May Day as Mayday, given that the inquest was certain to send distress signals in my direction...

The actual date of the inquest had already proved to be a slight bone of contention, so to speak. When the coroner's official phoned to tell me the date which had been set for the hearing, I at once informed her of its proximity to our wedding anniversary, but this was summarily brushed aside (only a few weeks before he died, Tom had suggested a return visit to Venice for that particular anniversary celebration). On reflection, I realised that in fact the date was rather appropriate, since the day of the inquest would presumably bring the marriage to a final, legal ending, verified by the issue of a full death certificate.

But first I would have to deal with the coroner's questions. In his quest for convenient answers the coroner would, I knew, be searching for a reason not just in the suicide note itself, but in the undated letter over which the detective had quizzed me so relentlessly. However, my solicitor was perfectly happy for me to attend the inquest unaccompanied, saying that after the way in which I'd already dealt with the detective and with my husband's employers, I could safely be left to deal with the coroner by myself, too. I took that as an enormous compliment!

None of which prevented my feelings of apprehension as the appointed day approached. I prepared myself as thoroughly as I could, reading through all the relevant documents and doing my best to view it as just another business meeting, although it was obviously going to be harrowing, to say the least. The suicide note would be unpleasant going in itself, of course, but the police had consistently tried to insist that the undated letter had a bearing on my husband's suicide, which was not only untrue but also extremely painful. And that was the main reason why I felt so strongly that I must attend alone, since I had my solicitor's approval to do so – I had no wish to distress anyone else any further. My sons had each offered to accompany me if that had been what I wanted, but I could tell that neither of them relished the prospect, understandably. And to see them put through that additional pain would be heartbreaking for me. Similarly, I saw no reason to involve my brother or any of my friends. This had already begun to feel like my own personal battle with my late husband, with my reputation at stake, and I preferred to fight that battle alone.

I dressed with great care. As irrelevant and even flippant as that may initially seem on an occasion of such desperate sadness, it was, of course, intended purely to give myself confidence. In my smart leather attaché case – a corporate gift from my City days, many years previously – I carried all the relevant paperwork together with a few items which I had removed from my husband's current briefcase, long after the police had finished with it.

These included a book of cheque stubs dated 1992, letters concerning investments from the late-90s and a British Airways Clubcard which had expired in 2001. I had chosen these, and a few other items, to support my claim that the contents of my husband's current briefcase were not necessarily current. Including the now infamous undated letter. I also carried a print of the final photo of Tom: standing beside me, our arms around each other and laughing into the camera, on Christmas Day – just four days before he was going to commit suicide. As an afterthought I added my digital camera, so that I could, if necessary, prove the date of the photo, if the coroner should choose to disbelieve my word about the date of that, too.

Approaching the reception desk in the Crown Court building alongside the police station, I was stopped and my bag searched. My camera caused a degree of alarm which would have been amusing if the occasion had not been so serious. The camera was instantly confiscated: mildly, I enquired about a receipt, which was then slapped down onto the reception desk. I thanked the official, graciously I hoped, and received a nod and a grunt in reply. I found my way to the waiting area where, disappointingly, no manacled criminals presented themselves to my gaze as they waited for the full wrath of the law to be brought down upon them. No weeping witnesses; and more importantly as far as I was concerned, no members of the Press. Presumably my husband's death ranked as simply yet another sordid little tale of suicide, of no interest even to local reporters. I was hugely relieved.

The next person to approach me was the coroner's official who had been present on that nightmarish evening, and had supervised both the investigation of the 'scene' and the removal of my husband's body. She complimented me on my appearance; as I followed her, I began to wonder whether that, too, might count against me, in this judicial world where, as my experience to date had taught me, nothing is as it seems, and no one should be taken at face value...

I handed over to her the items which I had brought from my late husband's briefcase, explaining briefly their relevance to the proceedings. She took them without comment, simply assuring me that she would pass them on to the coroner. Then, in the absence of any other usher, she ushered me in to the court itself, and left me. I was determined to take a perfectly detached interest in my surroundings: if only to pass the time. The large, light room was fitted in a thoroughly modern style and with all the latest communication equipment, yet retained the traditional atmosphere, evidently designed to intimidate, with its steeply tiered layout.

At the lowest level was a vast array of wooden seating for such attendees as myself. This resembled a school classroom from my own childhood, with a length of plain desk in front of each row of hard seats. I deliberately chose my seat in the front row: although I might look lost in that empty space, I was determined not to look lost in the eyes of the law! Above me was an area of desks and seating, with computer screens, for occupation by the various court officials, with the witness box to one side. Above that, at the highest level, naturally, and directly beneath the Royal Coat of Arms, were situated the richly padded and decorated seats befitting the presiding Officers of the Crown.

There was no minor official present to announce 'All Rise' (or All of me Rise, in this case, as I was seated in solitary state), but I thought it would be courteous to do so anyway. I received in response only a curt nod from the man who now entered and took his place directly beneath the royal insignia. The initial impression was of an unprepossessing man who could quite easily pass unnoticed as any small-town solicitor or bank manager of a slightly old-fashioned variety. He was followed by that same official with whom I had dealt throughout, and who now took her place at one of the slightly lowlier desks, with a suitably deferential air.

Once established in his seat of authority, the coroner seemed to expand to fill his appointed role. Graciously, he informed his official that she would not be required to take the oath for this particular hearing, as she had already done so earlier in the day; that would suffice. However, in my capacity as a witness, I would certainly be required to do so. I stood once again, and concentrated on speaking in measured tones, determined to keep my voice clear, calm and strong.

And so the hearing proceeded, and was all as cold and heartless as I had expected. The coroner stated at the outset that the object of the hearing was to establish the facts concerning the identity of the deceased and the means by which he met his death, but was:

"Not to apportion blame."

The coroner then displayed an apparent intention to apportion blame, by mounting a sustained attack on me over the undated letter, which he apparently persisted in believing to have been written shortly before my husband's death, and therefore to have had a direct bearing on his suicide. Asked whether there had been any warning signs of my husband's intention to commit suicide, or anything unusual in his behaviour on the morning of his death, I could only quote my husband's answer to my enquiry that lunchtime, about his plans for the rest of the day:

"I'm going to have a rest this afternoon."

The coroner made no comment on that. In his view, it still seemed to leave the undated letter as the only possible explanation: that my husband's suicide should remain inexplicable was not, apparently, an option.

The coroner decided that the letter could not be three years old, since such an old document would not have been in a currently-used briefcase. This struck me as being tantamount to accusing me of lying, and therefore presumably of perjury, since I was giving evidence under oath. I referred the coroner to the items which I had extracted from the briefcase and handed to his official. He judiciously informed me that I could not have taken those items from the briefcase because if, as I claimed, my husband kept everything, the briefcase would have been, in the learned gentleman's words:

"A foot and a half high."

In response, I attempted to remind the coroner that I had not claimed my husband kept everything in the briefcase: merely that he kept everything, an apparently random selection of which had been found in his current briefcase. However, the coroner interrupted me and would not allow me to finish my statement, denying me the chance to defend myself against his direct attack upon me. To attack but to allow no defence does not, in my opinion, constitute justice.

This apparent tactic of intimidation was immediately employed again, as the coroner now quizzed me on the actual contents of the undated letter, and the argument to which it referred. Being obliged to go into personal details about the nature of the row itself, I attempted to put my side of the case but was again interrupted, as the coroner told me peremptorily:

"I am not interested."

There followed personal questions, to my mind both irrelevant and impertinent, including a direct question on the state of the marriage. Given the extremely 'grave' nature of the occasion, I refrained from retorting that had the state of the marriage been in question, surely I should have been appearing in a divorce court, not a coroner's court. All these questions were fired at me relentlessly, with no hint of compassion and no concern for the potential effects of such an interrogation on me, as the widow and the sole non-official witness. And this, from a coroner who had opened the proceedings by stating that the object of the hearing was:

"Not to apportion blame."

I rest my case.

The coroner's questioning of myself as witness was followed by his official's providing full and graphic details of the exact position of the body in the garage, its condition on removal, the results of the post-mortem, and the self-tightening nature of the running knots used by the deceased to ensure the efficiency of the noose. The official's tone was utterly impassive and impersonal, as though she were describing a piece of meat on a slab. Her manner struck me as being geared purely to suit the dictatorial style of the coroner, with no acknowledgement of my presence, as the widow and as the discoverer of the body. I concentrated on keeping my own features impassive, and forced myself to continue taking notes in a businesslike fashion. Apparently the body contained no signs of any disease, and no trace of alcohol or any type of drug. Clearly, then, my husband had been determined to take this action and had needed no artificial assistance to carry it out.

The verdict was of course suicide, though *not* whilst of unsound mind, since the coroner found:

"No evidence of depression or any other illness which could have triggered his action. The deceased knew exactly what he was doing."

On seeing the coroner's official in the waiting area afterwards, I made her aware of my total dissatisfaction with the proceedings. I was merely informed that should I wish to lodge a complaint, the first part of the procedure would be for me to pay the court £40 simply to provide me with a transcript of the hearing. And that would have been only the beginning. I immediately decided, as I waited for the return of my confiscated camera, that I had more important matters with which to occupy my mind and my finances. I collected my camera and left.

But the inquisitorial nature of the proceedings, and the imperiously judgmental attitude of the coroner (who was not, of course, actually a judge) would prove to be a major setback in my recovery. Its result was simply to provide further fuel for the insidiously growing flame of anger against my husband – the man who had placed me in this hideous position in the first place, however inadvertently.

In the meantime, pausing on the flight of concrete steps outside the Crown Court, I drew deep breaths of fresh air while the coroner's conclusion swirled in my brain.

"The deceased knew exactly what he was doing."

Indeed. Such was the verdict of the law, leaving me with the inescapable conclusion that my late husband was in full command of his faculties, and therefore of his actions, when he emptied our accounts, when he somehow got rid of his computer to cover his financial tracks, and, finally, when he put the noose around his neck. And since, according to the legal verdict, he was apparently *not* of unsound mind, he would also have known who must find him, and how.

I had heard of a recent suicide in the same circumstances, except in that case, the deceased had left a prominently positioned note in the house for his wife, which read:

"Phone the police and don't go into the garage."

If the coroner was correct in his assertion that my husband knew exactly what he was doing, then he had obviously not shown any such consideration for me. On the contrary, it would seem that my husband had been coldly determined to involve his wife in his own destruction, and was fully cognizant of the effects of his actions on those whom he had once loved.

Alone and unseen outside the Crown Court, I pulled off my wedding and engagement rings and tossed them into my attaché case with vehement disdain. I would never wear them again.

Chapter 14: Fault lines

In the wake of the inquest, and especially in view of the coroner's extremely unhelpful and unsympathetic comments, my anger against my dead husband flared up even more strongly, taking serious hold of my heart, my mind and my imagination. Perhaps bereavement by suicide rarely, if ever, feels like a 'normal' grieving process, but the growing intensity of my anger soon came to overwhelm the more natural process of grieving for my husband. And so it became increasingly difficult to separate my anger from my very real, raw grief, and to allow myself to remember Tom as he had been, through all our years together: the real Tom. The memory of his innate kindness – his goodness, in fact – was slipping away from me, and for many months I was content to let it go: in comparison with the horror of his final act, it no longer seemed to matter.

Anger feeds on adrenaline, of course, and I was aware that I couldn't live on adrenaline indefinitely, unless I wanted to end up seriously ill. And that was not to be contemplated; I now felt as though I were in the middle of a battle, albeit a battle with a dead man, and I would need every ounce of my strength if I were successfully to wrest control of my life from his shadow and to win back my peace of mind.

But still the anger blazed, and still the adrenaline flowed. And yet I knew, of course, that the coroner's verdict was completely at odds with the medical verdict. Our own GP's opinion was straightforward: my husband had been suffering from undiagnosed depression. Despite the complete absence of any noticeable warning signs, perhaps some of the symptoms were there after all and, more disturbingly, always had been: acute sensitivity to criticism; the need to feel in control; the belief that any admission of self-doubt, or of a need for help, could signify only weakness and failure. In Tom's particular circumstances, I now felt there were other factors which I must add to that already formidable list: his looming retirement (three years away when he died) and consequent reduction in not only income, but even in activity and a sense of purpose; the intense and ever-increasing stress levels at work in the meantime; and his lifelong inability to confide in anyone.

Tom had never had any real friends of his own. He was close to his cousin, but other than that one lifelong relationship, he had always relied almost exclusively on his parents' ideals and opinions. Throughout the thirty-one years of our marriage, apart from Tom's cousin all 'our' friends had actually been my friends. His mother had been the bedrock of the family and its chief decision-maker, and had died almost twenty years previously; his father had lived on alone and died only four years before Tom himself. It struck me in hindsight that Tom had probably never recovered from the loss of his parents; without them, his life must have seemed rudderless. I remembered how shocked I had felt at hearing Tom's almost unearthly wail, on seeing his dead father (whose elderly body had quite simply worn out) in the hospital bed, and how Tom had shaken and sobbed uncontrollably. I began to realise now, after the manner of Tom's own death, that he must have felt more than even the usual grief at the loss of an elderly parent; with both his beloved parents gone, Tom might quite conceivably have lost his way completely.

Throughout his life, Tom had always demanded complete perfection from himself (though not, it must be said, from others), which led him to set his own standards incredibly high. If he fell short of his own ideal by, say, one notch, that seemed to him to be no better than falling short by ten notches, or even by a hundred notches: he had still fallen short. And that, in his polarised view of himself, meant failure, which in turn would have meant a loss of self-respect and another shift in his view of his place in the world, and in the lives of the people around him.

All these factors must have played their part, as the darkness of depression closed in on him and his mind began its tumultuous and unchecked descent into complete disintegration. As a function of his own character Tom would never, at any stage, have allowed himself to relax, to be caught off guard, or to admit – even to himself – that anything was wrong. And meanwhile, all the many good things in his life must have been slipping relentlessly out of his grasp, until the force of the depression which was consuming him would have stretched so unbearably taut that, finally, it snapped: imploding within his mind and destroying all reason.

The medical view was that catastrophic and irreversible chemical changes would have taken place within the brain itself at that point. All sense of balance must then have disappeared completely, leaving only a void of churning chaos, where nothing made sense any longer and normal life seemed to be lived out, by everyone except himself, on the other side of an impenetrable glass screen: a normality still visible to him and yet totally inaccessible. The mental torture which must have been caused by those feelings of intense despair remained completely unimaginable to me. Normal human emotions – particularly love, self-respect and consideration for the feelings of others – must then have become nothing more than the vaguest of intangible memories, or perhaps they had already passed entirely out of his reach, as though they had never existed.

On a purely mental and neurological basis, I could readily accept all this reasoning, yet the medical explanation seemed to me to retain an element of supposition, given Tom's complete lack of symptoms. He had never been obviously nervous or neurotic, but quite the opposite; always strong and decisive; plus, of course, he had seemed positively happy on the evening before his death, at our quiet and relaxed post-Christmas drinks party. But perhaps, in the dark and terrifyingly inverted logic of suicide, that was because by then his decision had already been taken. He would end his life the following day, so that release from his mental torment, final and blissful release, had become reassuringly imminent. In a mind so totally warped out of all reasoned function, and with all normal emotions now hopelessly out of reach, that prospect of release, or perhaps of complete oblivion, must have risen out of the darkness as the ultimate comfort: his own personal view of paradise after a seething, living hell.

And yet: how could I possibly reconcile these clinical and logical explanations with the final actions of the man who had once loved and cherished his family? The accepted view is that in a suicidal mind, anger and loathing are directed against the self.

Therefore, in this case, surely there must have been something more, to cause my husband to direct his anger and vindictiveness outwards, towards me, in his apparent determination to make my circumstances as difficult as possible after his death.

These feelings of having been utterly rejected by my life's partner were perhaps the hardest to bear, and therefore the first to be consigned to the flames of my own anger. Try as I would to view his actions towards me as simply another facet of his final mental breakdown, I could not put aside the unanswerable, if perhaps selfish, question which I longed to scream at my dead husband: *How could you do this to us – to me?*

But any attempt to fathom the answer to that question for myself was futile, of course, since it involved me in normal reasoning, and clearly Tom's suicidal mind would by that stage have moved completely beyond the reach of all reason.

And what of our sons? Who can possibly take the place of a father, and how could these two young men begin to deal with the knowledge that their father, their role model, had committed this terrible act of self-destruction, and with it the devastation of the family stability which had been the bedrock of their lives? Surely, I reasoned, if their father had been in his right mind he would never have contemplated inflicting such profound harm on them, whatever his feelings towards me may have become. That consideration, coupled with his apparent vindictiveness, led me to tell myself that once his feelings for himself were such that death seemed preferable to life, my husband could not by then have retained the slightest concern for the feelings of anyone else.

Despite these attempts to view Tom's descent towards suicide from a rational perspective, I struggled for many months with a certain amount of guilt: had I done something to *deserve* our family life being brought crashing down on the heads of us all? Could I have prevented his suicide? Surely, as the person closest to him, I should have noticed that something was wrong, and therefore, equally surely, I should have been able to save him... Those questions tortured me during the days, and more especially the nights, when the feelings of guilt would creep painfully into my waking thoughts and my restless nightmares.

But gradually, as the extent of his financial machinations became clear and the anger took hold, other and more practical considerations obliterated such unanswerable questions and unhealthy lines of thought. Because another of the accepted views concerning suicide is that, in the much earlier stages of depression, it is absolutely vital to seek help *before* those feelings of despair begin to turn insidiously into feelings of suicide. Of course someone with depression prefers to retreat into a protective, personal shell: therefore it would have taken courage to emerge from that shell far enough and long enough to seek help.

There were inevitably two opposing schools of thought being discussed in the village after Tom's death: to commit suicide is an act of cowardice; to end one's own life is an act of courage. Yes, of course it is possible consciously to end one's own life in an act of courage:

"Greater love hath no man than this; that he lay down his life for his friends," as the Bible says.

But a suicide does not lay down his own life for another; he does not dash into the road to save a child, or take aid to a part of the world stricken by deadly disease, or break cover under fire to rescue a comrade-in-arms. No: it would seem that in the tortured and broken mind of a suicide, the prospect of continuing life is quite simply even more terrifying than the prospect of imminent death. And that, in my opinion at least, does not constitute courage.

So my own conclusion was that there must have been a time when Tom could have sought help. Even when the idea of suicide crept into his mind for the very first time, perhaps hinting at its presence by the merest whisper, he must surely have realised that such a thought is not a normal reaction to stress or inner turmoil, but represents the most urgent alarm signal, calling for immediate help. And that, of course, would have meant talking to someone. Anyone. Something which Tom would never do. And so, instead of acknowledging that to seek support is not a sign of weakness but of courage, he allowed the process of disintegration to begin. The cracks in his mind must then have widened until they formed an impassable chasm between himself and the rest of the world, cutting him off completely.

It was precisely that lack of courage to admit to the need for help, coupled with the calculated dispersal of our joint funds, which had first ignited my anger against my dead husband. And as I turned my seemingly inescapable conclusion over in my mind, time and again, it fed the flames of my anger until I felt as though my heart and mind were being engulfed in a raging inferno of the most intense emotions I had ever experienced. But how was I to deal with such surging emotions, for the sake of my own short-term relief and longer-term health? I was painfully aware that I had a huge quantity of excess baggage to handle. The physical baggage of my late husband's possessions was compounded by that of his parents and bedridden aunt, which between them comprised a large stack of house-moving boxes. But more importantly, I was also carrying a massive amount of emotional baggage, the lot of the survivor after a marriage which has been ended by the violence of suicide.

The physical baggage was the easier variety to handle; in fact, dealing with it was therapeutic. There's nothing like physical exercise for working through strong emotion, and I felt rather like the proverbial wronged wife who dumps her erring husband's possessions on the street, for all the neighbours to see. Except that in my case, there was no one to see, as I transported sack load after hefty sack load of clothing and motorbike gear to the nearest charity shops, and car load after back-breaking car load of possessions to the council tip. Old rusted bicycles belonging to Tom and his father; his grandfather's building tools and working overalls; defunct electrical equipment including the first-ever computer game – tennis played with white dots and pinging noises – from the early 1980s; the list went on. From his parents' stock, carefully labelled in Tom's handwriting, there were large boxes of dusty ornaments and vases, chipped china animals won at fairgrounds, several tea sets, endless linens, unused sets of saucepans still with their price tags in pounds, shillings and pence, an unused, galvanised steel dustbin; that list, too, went on. I sold as much as I could, mainly the larger items such as the two desks and two filing cabinets from Tom's study, our rowing boat with outboard engine, his mother's two sewing machines...

Meanwhile the paper shredder was kept busy, too, with items such as every payslip dating back to the 1970s, every paper relating to every tax return, and every out-of-date tax disc for every vehicle Tom had ever owned. He could not, indeed, ever relinquish his hold on anything. But gradually, as I became more used to taking all decisions and all responsibility alone, and as I even started to plan for the redecoration of Tom's rapidly emptying study, I began to feel I was regaining control of more than just my physical surroundings: I was starting to regain control of my life.

The emotional baggage was proving harder to dispose of than the physical variety, or at least harder to gauge in its effects. I refused to allow myself to dwell on those feelings of guilt which, in any case, tended to be swept aside by the continuing wave upon wave of anger. But I knew I had to be careful, if I were to avoid a slide into bitterness, or even – ghastly thought – into depression myself. So I continued to see lifelong friends whenever possible, and to go on occasional trips with local friends to the theatre or concerts. I found myself turning down as many invitations as I accepted, largely because these trips were a luxury which was becoming more than my seriously-reduced budget could stand. But I continued to smile and laugh, however much I secretly hated being the add-on; the woman on her own. This was all a completely new situation for me, having been with Tom all my adult life, and I began to experience the truth of the saying that the middle of a crowd can be the loneliest place of all.

My greatest source of comfort and support remained my family and small circle of close friends, while in times of solitude my inexhaustible supply of consolation and pleasure was reading. I continued to choose my reading material extremely carefully during those first few months, particularly my bedtime reading, of course. This largely comprised old favourites such as Arthur Ransome's *Swallows and Amazons* stories, and well-loved humour such as P G Wodehouse's *Jeeves* series. Books which not only fulfilled my very real need to be transported out of myself, but which had always been such a familiar part of my life that to open the covers felt like being comforted by old friends. And so I would open a favourite volume and feel that I was simply disappearing inside as the familiar characters and the rhythm of the well-loved words drew me in, enveloping me like an embrace until I was oblivious to everything else, however briefly.

Favourite classic novels and poetry, modern novels and short stories; all played their part in shoring me up. I also read a wider variety of biographies and memoirs than I'd ever done before, mainly those of strong, independent women who had faced their own crises, of whatever description. Foremost among these, I reread *The Diary of Anne Frank* for the umpteenth time, emerging humbled and stricken, yet heartened and strengthened for my own situation, as I'd known I would be.

I continued my lifelong diary-writing habit, keeping a careful record of feelings as well as events, and I regularly wrote emails and letters to friends in which I would delight in chronicling the absurdities arising out of my situation, insofar as any delight was possible in my particular circumstances. But writing about everything that had happened was making it not only easier to accept mentally, but gradually easier to bear emotionally, too. I was, in fact, beginning to write my own personal part of this tragedy out from the deepest recesses of my own mind, and therefore also from my heart.

By being brought out into the daylight, confronted, and then turned into words, the horror was starting to dissipate; and with it my grief, my emptiness, and my fear for the future. And, perhaps most importantly for my own wellbeing, my intense anger against Tom himself: wherever he might be now. That tricky question of where he might be now was one which I had not allowed to occupy too much of my attention. I felt that the sheer impact of his suicide and the practicalities surrounding it were distressing enough, without contemplating any additional unanswerable questions.

I had been brought up in the Church of England, to believe in the promise of a continuing spiritual existence. That concept of some form of ongoing presence quite naturally brings immeasurable comfort to bereaved believers, especially during the early days of intense mourning. Perhaps it even brings a feeling that the dead can somehow be watching over the living, and therefore still caring, with their innate character still comfortingly intact. But this was certainly not the case for me, given the apparent contempt in which my husband held me at the time of his death. Of course, that contempt was itself a function of the disintegration of his mind, and yet I was left with the bleak knowledge that he died caring nothing for his family. And so any comfort of believing in his continuing existence was completely unknown to me.

Rather surprisingly, perhaps, a full Church of England funeral can still be refused in the case of a suicide, under ancient Church law which is only now due to be changed. Under this law, the official funeral service is not supposed to be used where 'the person deceased ... being of sound mind have laid violent hands upon himself.' Interestingly then, in the light of the coroner's verdict at the inquest into my husband's death, ancient Church law would appear to agree with modern secular law, in decreeing that it is possible to commit suicide whilst of sound mind. I found this concept extremely difficult to reconcile with the circumstances surrounding Tom's death, and with the devastating change in personality which was implied if he had, in fact, been completely sane as he coldly and meticulously planned both his suicide and its consequences for his family.

In reality, of course, that particular provision of Church of England law has long been completely ignored by its clergy, who would not nowadays uphold such an unsympathetic and outmoded view of someone who had decided, for whatever reason, to take his (or her) own life. Certainly the clergy in the village were outstandingly kind and sympathetic, and as deeply shocked and distressed as everyone else. There was never any doubt that my husband was just as entitled to the full rites of the Church as anyone else. In fact, the clergy's genuine care and concern were self-evident as they did everything in their power to offer practical, as well as spiritual, help and support to my family and myself. Their immediate concern was for the living rather than the dead, and at no time did I feel that the clergy, or indeed any other member of the Church, presumed to pass judgment on suicide.

Despite all these considerations – or perhaps because of them – it seemed to me that the question of where my husband might be now was an interesting and absorbing one, which simply invited some rather irreverent speculation...

Chapter 15: The sublime to the ridiculous

He didn't know how it had happened, really. One moment he'd been staring down through a square hole into churning chaos, then there'd been a falling, and a breathless hush; and now here he was.

Those gates ahead of him must be the Pearly Gates themselves, he supposed, though as far as he could tell they weren't so much pearly as a sort of iridescent wrought iron. Several distinct queues of people were being ushered, by immense figures in white robes, along a walkway of shifting clouds which led towards the gates. The scene reminded him strongly of an airport, and, as if on cue, he suddenly noticed the overhead sign: *Welcome to the Astral Plane*. He found himself in a line of new arrivals making its sedate way towards an information desk, where another of the white-robed figures appeared to be directing each newcomer to the appropriate queue for the gates. Beyond the gates stood another well-ordered group of people, whose faces were aglow with delighted anticipation as they awaited the imminent arrival of their loved ones.

"*Tom!*" yelled a well-remembered voice, cutting sharply through the calm and causing a nearby angel to wince slightly. "Look, Ern – it's Tom!"

And there she was; his own dear mother, waving wildly and calling excitedly from the other side of the gates.

"*Tom!* What on Earth d'you think you're doing?"

"But Mum, I don't think I'm on Earth any more: am I?"

" 'Course you're not, you're standing at the Gates of Heaven, but you're not supposed to be up 'ere for ages yet. *Ern!*"

"What's up, Pam?"

And there was his father, ambling towards his mother while carefully closing a pair of golden secateurs and stowing them lovingly in the capacious pocket of his overalls. He peered myopically through the park-like gates.

"Ah, Tommy-boy, so you've arrived, then. Good. I need you to help me with pruning all them roses in the Celestial Gardens. I was just saying to Percy Thrower, it's about time we got some new apprentices. But he's a good boss, is Percy, and what he don't know about blackfly on roses..."

At this point the touching family reunion was brought to an abrupt halt, hushed by an usher.

"All shall be revealed in due season," prophesied the ushering angel, as Tom found himself approaching the information desk, while his parents' voices receded into a comforting background hum.

"Welcome to the arrival Gates. Name and date of death, please."

Tom responded, registering slight surprise at how natural it felt to give his latest details.

"Ah, yes: a suicide. I've got you on my list."

Coming in like a well-trained chorus, several angelic figures now bent towards Tom and murmured a soft greeting in soothing four-part harmony.

"I'll get someone to escort you, as suicides qualify for one-to-one assistance."

Immediately, one of the angelic figures stood before him, smiling reassuringly. This, then, was his very own personal Assistant Angelic Usher, wearing a conspicuously large badge (*AAU: Here to Help*) and gliding gently beside him as Tom took his place at the end of what appeared to be rather a slow-track queue.

Suddenly, Tom heard a distant and agonised scream, apparently coming from somewhere far below him and piercing the clouds at his feet. Looking down, he noticed that the clouds seemed to be thinning, as if in response to that scream, and through their swirling mistiness he saw – his wife. He'd never heard her scream before. Not in all those years. She was standing in a garage, beside a car – his own sports car, surely? – with her head thrown back, staring upwards at something, the horror in her eyes visible even from up here. And, his vision still somewhat clouded by mistiness, there *she* was, too: Misty, alone in a familiar-looking house, just barking, barking...

"Ah well," thought Tom, turning away as the clouds once more thickened beneath him to shut out both that vision and that cacophony of alarm, "someone else can sort that out, whatever it is. After all, I couldn't be expected to carry on multi-tasking forever. I deserve a rest."

Nevertheless, it was with a slightly uncomfortable sensation that Tom turned his attention to his surroundings; just to pass the time, as the heavenly wait did seem to be infernally long.

"You are currently being held in a queue," intoned the loudspeaker, in a suitably grave manner of speaking, "and will be transferred to the next available Angelic Advisor. Your soul is important to us: we are doing all we can to minimise waiting times, and we apologise for any inconvenience."

As he looked beyond the queue and through the partially-open gates, a varied and colourful scene presented itself to Tom's eyes. Voices floated towards him over angelic heads; snatches of conversation were flowing down like crystal waters. On a wide, sunlit greensward a young woman, clad in a full suit of mediaeval armour, was evidently holding her audience spellbound. (Her inquisitors, had they been privileged to be present, would no doubt have claimed that this merely served to prove their point about heresy.)

"That's St Joan of Arc," Tom's Usher told him, following the direction of his gaze. "She always draws huge crowds; particularly the French, of course. And that," – indicating an elderly gentleman sitting at St Joan's feet, avidly scribbling her words into a large notebook and casting occasional adoring glances at her – "is George Bernard Shaw. He never misses any of her speeches."

"I was not in my right mind till I was free of the body," declaimed St Joan, her hands clasped together in girlish glee, to general nods and smiles of approval from the congregation.

Unfortunately, the girlish glee aspect was slightly impaired by the clashing together of the enormous pair of armour-plated gauntlets, in which her hands were also clasped. But to his very great surprise, Tom found himself nodding his own approval of her words, too, which seemed to be having the most extraordinary effect in clearing his mind. He was beginning to realise that it had become rather cluttered, just lately.

His Angelic Usher was smiling at Tom, knowingly.

"Once we've completed all the formalities and got your particulars registered onto the iCloud, I'll give you full details of our programme of events. Actually, you've arrived at a very good time: we have some excellent speakers lined up. St Cecelia is due to give a lecture entitled *The Biblical operas: fact or fiction?* It's sure to be popular, 'specially as it includes a heavenly picnic on the Celestial Lawns. Oh yes," – consulting an impressively long list – "and St Francis is shortly going to speak on *Feathers and Flappers: clothing the birds*. No doubt that'll be even more popular."

Tom shook his head at the idea of attending any lecture by St Francis, shuddering slightly as he remembered not only Misty's recent frantic barking, but also Jerry the tortoise, still in mid-hibernation in the fridge. Oh well, someone else would have to sort that out, too. At least he'd weighed Jerry – was it really only this morning? – and carefully added the latest details to the hand-written health chart. He hadn't put the information on the computerised version this time, as he hadn't wanted his laptop to be left lying around after his...departure. He'd got rid of the laptop somehow, although for some reason he couldn't quite remember where... Tom wrenched his attention back to what his AAU was saying.

"...and then there's to be a debate on the superiority (or otherwise) of women drivers, chaired by St Catherine, *Wheels;* the sparks are bound to fly at that one!"

Chuckling slightly at this divine witticism, his Usher proceeded to ask Tom what his own particular interests had been on Earth. Tom thought for a moment: he'd always been so busy down there on Earth that, looking back, he wasn't sure he'd had time for anything much in the way of interests; apart from work, of course. Then he brightened.

"I used to help run a motorbike club," he said, tentatively. "At least, in the last few years I seemed to spend more time working on the club's website and dealing with online queries than riding motorbikes, but I got that club running much more efficiently. Perhaps there's something similar up here?"

His Angelic Usher seemed unsure.

"I'll certainly look into it for you, Tom, but I can't promise. There may turn out to be insufficient numbers for a motorbike club up here, as the Hell's Angels are all engaged elsewhere..."

They were now near enough to the gates for Tom to notice that some sort of repair work seemed to be going on along one section. Once again, his Angelic Usher appeared to read Tom's thoughts.

"Yes, we've had to call in the builders to see to the hinges again – all that swirling mass of cloud really does take a toll. They've been busy with the bells, too, for the same reason."

"My grandfather was a builder on Earth: d'you think he might...?"

Tom broke off for a moment, almost overcome at the idea of seeing Grandad again, after all this time. "His surname is – was – Hawkins."

His Usher hailed a nearby angel holding a large clipboard, and enquired after Mr Hawkins. No, he wasn't working on the gates, but there was certainly a Mr Hawkins just on the other side.

"You're in luck," said the angel with the clipboard, after consulting it briefly, "It seems that Robert Louis Stevenson has been 'specially commissioned to re-write Jim Hawkins back from Treasure Island, to help with a rather delicate issue. Yes, look, that's him over there; coming alongside three late Archbishops of Canterbury, as they're all still very much at See over the ordination of women bishops."

"No, no!" cried Tom, "Not *Jim* Hawkins – *Jack* Hawkins. He was a builder in the mortal life, not a sailor."

The angel with the clipboard consulted it once more.

"Ah yes, Jack Hawkins the builder; he's over there too, as it happens, helping the three Graces with their mitre joints..."

At that moment, they all looked round as a lady, dressed in a delicately flowing muslin gown, joined the oddly assorted assembly and made her obeisance to the Archbishops of Canterbury.

"Oh good, Jane Austen's arrived."

The angel with the clipboard heaved a sigh of relief.

"She was invited most particularly, you know, with the aim of bringing both Sense and Sensibility to Their Graces' deliberations."

"What are men to rocks and mountains?" enquired Miss Austen rhetorically, in tones of gentle Persuasion. "It is a truth universally acknowledged, that the extent of men's Pride and Prejudice remains undiminished."

Tom was beginning to feel slightly bemused.

"Come on, Tom," said his Usher encouragingly, "We'll have you through the gates in no time now, and then you'll be able to rejoin all your dear family."

"Oh, my Sainted Aunt!"

The well-known voice carried across to Tom once more, like a clarion call.

"Where, Mum?" Tom called back excitedly, swinging round. "And which aunt?"

Which of his several aunts, great-aunts and now, apparently, even-greater-aunts, could it possibly be? *Sainted?* What an honour! Perhaps it would be Great Auntie Mabel, in recognition of all those Christmas presents she used to provide for the entire family, year after year... He turned to his Angelic Usher, more animated now than that particular celestial being had yet seen him.

"Is it a bit like being knighted, only more so?"

"Well, it's certainly a wonderful experience," replied his Usher with the ghost of a smile, "as St Joan is just about to attest, I believe. But I don't think that's quite what your mother means."

With that, and at a nod from the angel with the clipboard, Tom's Angel ushered him towards the very Gates of Heaven:

"This way, Tom. It is time."

"Oh no, it isn't!" cried his mother, with a note of authority in her voice: "You've got to get back down there and sort out that wife o' yours. Look what she's doing! She's chucked out all me best ornaments, what I told you to keep; she's..."

Here Tom's father cut in, attempting to soothe her.

"Now, Pam, you did die nearly twenty years ago," he reminded her, but to no avail, as her voice rose again in a peremptory:

"You get back down there, Tom!"

"But Mum, I don't think they'll let me go back," replied Tom, shooting a pleading glance at his Usher.

And besides, he added silently to himself, it might be a bit embarrassing. He was beginning to feel that he had no wish to explain his last mortal actions to anyone on Earth: certainly not to his own two sons, anyway. The Usher's head was shaking gently.

"No, Tom, such a return is not allowed, as you have already realised. What's done cannot be undone. Should you wish to join a discussion on such matters, though, I believe The Bard himself is to hold..."

But Tom's attention was now being claimed by his father who was, as usual, trying to sit on the fence. Though metaphorically rather than metaphysically in this instance, the heavenly gates being not only high, but also rather uncomfortably ornate in their topmost regions.

"Well, Tommy-boy, I think you'd better apply for one of them off-peak returns. Go and ask someone at that desk: tell 'em your mother says you've got to go back."

His mother, nodding vigorously, seemed about to launch into another tirade, but Tom's Angelic Usher was too quick for her, and glided forward authoritatively. As his parents' voices began to fade once more to a blessèd hum, Tom saw that the clouds beneath him were parting again, to reveal a sight which he knew instinctively would be his final glimpse of Earth.

There they all were: his wife, their two sons, his mother-in-law. Dressed in black, silent, but with their arms resolutely linked as though to form a chain. A human chain, unbroken and unbreakable.

He found himself moving gently through the gateway, as the clouds swirled into place beneath him once more. And as the Gates of Heaven closed softly behind him, Tom's father stepped forward to meet him, and placed a pair of golden secateurs into his hands.

Chapter 16: The tortoise and the care

Meanwhile, whatever might or might not be going on in other spheres, I had my own, purely earthly, matters to attend to. One of which was Jerry, our much-loved tortoise, who had continued to sleep his way peacefully through his hibernation, oblivious to the trauma which had engulfed the rest of the household.

While Misty the Westie had always been primarily 'my' pet, Jerry the Tortoise had been indisputably Tom's province. As much as I, too, had come to love that intriguing little creature and enjoyed feeding and taking care of him, with Tom there had been something more: a natural affinity. From childhood, Tom had always longed to own and care for a tortoise, and since a tortoise is by nature a quiet, withdrawn and essentially solitary creature, this really did seem to be a case of pets and their owners being temperamentally well-matched. I would look forward to my rambles with Misty, when I could enjoy the sights, sounds and smells of the countryside while letting my mind roam freely wherever it chose to go. Although Tom was perfectly happy to walk and play with the dog, he was noticeably more enthusiastic when it came to researching and absorbing all the technical data about tortoises, their life cycle and their care, including the most up-to-date hibernation technique, which is to place the sleeping tortoise into the controlled environment of – a fridge.

It turned out to be a major event in our family when we first 'met' Jerry, in Cornwall, and so that particular year can, perhaps, best be described as *2001: A Place Odyssey*. At that time we'd recently bought a holiday home on the north Cornwall coast, a small pre-fabricated bungalow with a narrow, slow-flowing stream at the end of the garden. We used to travel down from Hampshire to Cornwall as often as we could, all year round, the journey usually taking about three and a half hours. Mark and Paul adored their weekends and holidays in Cornwall, which led to both of them developing an abiding love of the coastal lifestyle.

One weekend during that first summer in Cornwall, Tom and I were removing debris from the stream after clearing our garden of some overgrown trees and bushes. To our momentary astonishment, we saw a stone moving in the sluggish water. Except it wasn't a stone, it was a small tortoise trying to climb up the steep bank. He was cold and clearly exhausted, with one front leg badly injured and almost useless. We took him straight to a vet, who operated on his leg immediately, and gave us a crash course in caring for this surprisingly endearing reptile, while we waited for someone to come forward and claim him. No one ever did, despite extensive enquiries in and around the village. The assumption had to be that he'd been living wild in our back garden, surviving on its vegetation and Cornwall's mild climate, and had tumbled into the stream when we'd suddenly set to work on his habitat. He was then aged about 80 or so, according to the vet, and wasn't microchipped.

We ended up keeping the tortoise, of course, and a clearly delighted Tom announced that he'd always wanted to call his tortoise Jerry. From then on Jerry came almost everywhere with us, as he was nearly blind due to cataracts and so he needed to be hand-fed daily. With his very own and very snug travelling box, he accompanied us not only to Cornwall, but to Yorkshire, Wales and even the Lake District. Jerry quickly became an experienced and quite nonchalant traveller!

Immediately after Jerry joined our household, Tom joined the Tortoise Trust, and learned all about nutrition, habitat and hibernation methods – including the details of reptilian refrigeration. The idea is to keep a constant and controlled hibernation temperature, and so avoid any risk of the tortoise waking up too early due to an unexpected rise in temperature. Apparently this is why, when I was a child and anyone lucky enough to own a tortoise would put it in a box of straw in the garden shed for the winter, fewer tortoises survived their hibernation: during a mild spell the tortoise could wake up and simply suffocate in its box. But once the tortoise has naturally stopped eating during the autumn, and processed the food still in its body, its metabolism slows down to a minimum level and the tortoise can then safely be placed in the fridge. At the optimum temperature of 6°C, the heartbeat will remain steady – at one beat per minute…

Jerry had his own personal fridge, which avoided the risk of anyone mistaking him for a Cornish pasty in the family-sized version! It was very useful, though, to be able to store a little extra food in Jerry's fridge sometimes, especially at Christmas; salad and fruit, naturally, to scent his dreams with the promise of spring. Jerry would be placed carefully into his fridge in mid-November, already asleep in his cardboard box lined with straw bedding. He had an old 'Cornish wildflowers' tea towel as his duvet, just to make sure he felt at home. Alongside Jerry in his box-bed, the fridge also contained a glass of water. This was not in case Jerry should get thirsty, but in case the fridge should get too warm and cause him to wake up. The glass of water had a thermometer in it, connected through the fridge door seal to a control panel with an alarm and a digital read-out panel, and a separate humidity indicator. I was always convinced that Jerry must have viewed this system rather like a panic button: he could rest assured (as it were) that if the temperature or the humidity inside the fridge should change, we humans would realise and could correct it for him. Tom even invested in our own small generator, so that in the event of winter power cuts, Jerry could stay safely asleep in his independently-run fridge.

When Misty joined our household as a puppy, she was at first terrified of this strange looking and strange smelling creature with a hard body and a tiny head; unusually terrified, for a terrier! She was slowly and carefully introduced to Jerry on supervised visits to his enclosed area of the garden, before coming with Tom or me at Jerry's feeding time, when she would lie quietly on the grass and watch him eat. Any perceived threat from Jerry as a competitor had obviously disappeared, once Misty realised that his diet bore absolutely no resemblance to her own. Gradually this unlikely pair became thoroughly used to each other, and would spend sunny afternoons snoozing side by side on the lawn, as Jerry now had the run (or the amble, really) of the whole garden in safety. When Jerry reappeared each spring after his winter sleep, Misty seemed in no way surprised to see him again, and remained completely relaxed in his company.

Owing to his poor eyesight, Jerry would very occasionally come to grief in the garden, turning himself over when misjudging his attempt to negotiate his way around an obstacle, and tipping himself over onto his back. He couldn't then right himself, owing to his dome-shaped shell, and Misty would come rushing to alert us, barking frantically.

The sight of Jerry on his back, legs flailing helplessly, was indeed an unnerving one. Once he had been righted, and Misty had gently sniffed him to check that he was unharmed, she would calm down. This overturning happened to Jerry only once or twice each summer, but whenever it did, it would produce exactly the same degree of alarm in Misty as it had done on the first occasion. On summer evenings, a part of Misty's routine was to help hunt around the garden to make sure Jerry had stowed himself safely somewhere, usually under a favourite bush. And on warm afternoons, I would enjoy seeing our two pets sharing a patch of dappled sunlight, the picture of companionable relaxation, and wonder whether they were, perhaps, even enjoying one another's company.

After Tom died, I made sure I maintained his well-established routine of regular health checks on Jerry, peacefully asleep in his fridge and in blissful ignorance. I weighed Jerry faithfully (that slight disturbance not being enough to wake him), and even wrote up the latest weekly details on the health chart Tom had first made so carefully back in 2001, and subsequently updated each winter. Tom would even enter the details onto his computer and print out weight graphs and charts. But adding my simple notes to his original hand-written and detailed ones was painful, as those sunlit memories would return each time, to pierce me afresh with their vivid clarity and feel, in hindsight, like an age of innocence.

When spring came round again, I eased Jerry out of hibernation and out of his fridge at the appropriate time, having been checking daily for the first signs of even the slightest movement in his straw bed. Somehow I lugged his large indoor pen into position, complete with his special reptile light and heat lamps on his very own overhead gantry, and then I secured the fencing around his outdoor pen as best I could. But I quickly realised that to care for him properly was simply too time-consuming, now that there was just the one of me. The garden at

Riverside wasn't yet tortoise-proof, as our garden in Fleet had been, and it posed many dangers to an almost-blind tortoise, the main one being, of course, the river. So I decided to have Jerry re-homed by the Tortoise Trust. It was not a decision I took lightly, but I knew I really had no choice.

On a very wet and gloomy day in late April, I drove Jerry and all his accoutrements – apart from the fridge itself – to a thoroughly tortoise-infested house in a quiet village in Surrey. Jerry's 'foster-carer' was kindness itself, and wanted to show me her vast family of tortoises, not realising what a painful occasion this was for me. Naturally I hated saying goodbye to Jerry; it brought on a bout of despondency which I found harder to shake off than I'd anticipated, and a return of that ghastly sense of unreality which I thought I'd left behind: a feeling that surely, this can't have happened to me, this unending and multi-faceted nightmare... But it simply made me realise that there could be no short cuts through my personal process of recovery; it was going to take time, effort and an awful lot of self-discipline.

After breaking his journey in Surrey, Jerry was to be taken to live with the Tortoise Trust's chairman in Wiltshire, until a permanent home could be found for him among the Trust's members. I kept in touch with the Trust's chairman, who was keen to assure me that Jerry was none the worse for his latest travels. In mid-summer I was told Jerry had finally moved to his permanent new home, where he was apparently settled and doing well, in – London!

I like to think of him as a rather suave tortoise-about-town now, especially after all the adventures he'd had during his twelve years with us. These had included the famous occasion of his being personally invited by a university vice-chancellor to attend a sample psychology lecture. Our Jerry, being an independent and incurably curious creature, proceeded to climb out of his travelling box and set off amongst the forest of legs in the lecture theatre, presumably intent on taking the podium himself. Jerry had also caused a stir when taking a stroll along a seaside promenade, where the members of a motorbike club, in conversation with Tom, had wanted to start up a 'Jerry's fan club' there and then...

In a strange way I loved that little creature as much as Tom did; watching and caring for Jerry taught me a great deal about perseverance and patience. But I have never doubted that my decision was the correct one for his sake; I'm simply glad that we had the care of Jerry the Tortoise for all those years.

While Jerry had chilled out and remained peacefully oblivious to the seismic crisis in the rest of the household, Misty quite naturally had not. Eight years old when Tom died, Misty had always been a healthy, happy dog. As I gradually learned to live alongside the memory and the effects of what had happened, I often wondered exactly what Misty had experienced, that day: wherever she was in the house, she was essentially separated from the garage by only one closed door. A dog's hearing being forty times more sensitive than a human's, would she have heard the inevitable noises, however brief they were, and realised what must be happening? Would she, in any case, have witnessed Tom's final preparations that afternoon, and sensed then that something was terribly wrong with him? Afterwards, she remained shut up alone in the empty and darkening house, and then had to endure the sights and sounds of strangers coming and going inside the house and garage – anathema to any dog, naturally – for two hours or more until the police and the coroner's official saw fit to de-restrict the house and allow Misty to be released. And then, on being brought next door to me, she obviously sensed my cataclysmic state. Perhaps her own state, on the other hand, should logically be described as dogaclysmic.

Misty's best friend in the village was Angela and John's dog, Poppy. After John was taken to hospital, where he died, Poppy would watch by the door, waiting patiently for him to come home. To my knowledge, Misty never once looked for Tom after his death. I remain convinced that however she arrived at her own canine understanding, Misty knew that the leader of her pack had gone off to die alone, just as sick or injured animals do.

In the immediate aftermath, Misty became noticeably more protective of me, and of the house. Front-door callers would invariably be greeted by her best Rottweiler impression, while the necessary trips to the garden last thing at night, and first thing in the morning, now involved her checking all the boundaries:

she would not come indoors until she was apparently satisfied that all was well. She continued to eat and sleep normally, but her appetite for playing with her toys indoors was gone. Apart from her walks, her chief pleasure was in playing ball in the garden; a game which she had always played only with me, whereas Tom and I had both been her indoor playmates.

Our outdoor and all-weather game is invariably played during the early afternoon, and is eagerly anticipated anytime from midday onwards. Called muzzleball, its necessary equipment consists of a hard medium-sized ball (Misty) and an old wooden lacrosse stick (me). The ball is first thrown from the stick (gently!) and as it lands it is leapt upon by Misty, who proceeds to charge at high speed across the 'pitch', pushing the ball with her muzzle and looking exactly as though she were intent on scoring a goal. The lacrosse stick, when I come running up behind her, panting like – well, a dog – is essential, not only for picking up the ball to throw it again without risk of losing a finger or two, but also for plunging in front of the current 'goal', usually a delicately-stemmed flower or a favourite shrub...

Misty is actually the undisputed Muzzleball World Champion, largely because nobody else is insane enough to play it, particularly in a very muddy garden in winter. So, when Misty lost interest in playing muzzleball, I knew she was ill. It had started with a stomach upset a few weeks after Tom died, which was hardly surprising. The vet prescribed the necessary medication and wasn't unduly concerned by her condition, so I didn't see any need to tell him what had recently happened in our household. Misty seemed to recover well, but the problem recurred a couple of months later, only now it was quite obviously worse. After various tests, the vet diagnosed a potentially serious problem. This time, I told him what had happened, and how it had involved Misty. The vet confirmed my instinctive feeling that Misty would have suffered her own canine version of trauma, in addition to her acute awareness of my emotions, which would naturally cause increased anxiety in any dog. The vet was taking her resulting condition very seriously; controlling it would involve putting Misty on a special veterinary diet for the rest of her life, and taking blood samples periodically.

I was only too glad that the problem could be controlled, as the health of my canine companion dwarfed my concern at the expense.

When Misty's next bout of illness flared up, the vet decided further investigation was warranted, involving a more comprehensive set of blood tests. At the same time, he decided to relieve the immediate symptoms by giving Misty an injection, and prescribed two sets of medication. (I almost needed medical assistance myself, when I saw the bill.) By now Misty was used to the routine, and was ready for the vet, plus the nurse, plus me hanging on to her sharp end. Misty doesn't give up her blood lightly, so the process involved three attempts, in both front legs and her neck. Though the odds were never in her favour, Misty put up a commendable fight against three humans: the vet rolled up his sleeves, the nurse was puffing and I had to take my jacket off. When we finally emerged, I was white and shaking – from the effects of the bill – while Misty was sporting a bright pink neck and two red bandages in front, the overall effect being as though she'd just gone a couple of rounds in the boxing ring. But I wasn't at all sure about the overall effect on the vet.

Misty had quite naturally become dearer than ever to me, now that she was my sole constant companion; the only other living being in the house, and my provider of affection, comfort, and a welcome. As her state of health became more fragile than it had ever been before Tom's death, my anger against him flared on behalf of our pets, too. Again, I knew that I must take steps to control that anger, as part of the need to take care of my own overall health.

Chapter 17: Owe dear me

Something within me had died on that dreadful day, an intangible yet profound part of me: the part which was inextricably linked with my husband. And so now I had to accept that my thirty-one year married life was over, and that I would need to nurture the fragile but still spirited part of me which remained, if that separate life of mine was to survive, to grow and develop, and even, ultimately, to thrive afresh. I had known from the start of my unrecognisably altered new life that I would owe it to myself, as well as to my family, to ensure there could be no question of succumbing to the mental and emotional stresses which had been thrust upon me, or to the potentially damaging physical results of those stresses.

As with the physical versus the emotional baggage left for me by my husband, the recovery of my physical health was easier to monitor than the emotional, and therefore simpler to deal with. The sedative prescribed by my doctor two days after Tom died had initially been increased, while I dealt with the immediate trauma and with the funeral itself. After a few weeks, though, the dose was gradually reduced, so that within three months I no longer needed it. I had been living in fear of becoming dependent on any form of sedative, however mild, and so I felt rather proud of myself when it became apparent to my doctor, as well as to me, that I was coping satisfactorily without that level of assistance. The only medication I needed during the following few months was a mild anti-histamine to help me settle at night, and I was able to dispense with even that by the middle of my first summer of living alone.

My doctor had warned me at the outset that some form of depressive reaction was bound to set in eventually, if not due to my sudden widowhood then at least to the shock of discovering my husband's body, and the manner of his death. The doctor felt it would be 'a miracle' if I didn't find myself needing anti-depressant medication at some stage during the process of learning to accept what had happened. Perversely, that statement had the effect of making me resolve to get through my recovery period without anything of the sort! And of course that, in turn, would require self-discipline, leading to self-control, leading to self-respect. All those aspects of my emotional wellbeing would be essential, I felt, if I were to emerge undamaged from the combined effects of shock, grief, anger and those feelings of guilt which would still insist on pushing their insidious way through my anger, particularly once that anger had begun to cool. But determination is a powerful motivating force, and I was determined to succeed.

The psychological effect of all my little victories became a major factor in my emotional recovery: everything from making myself use the garage again, to dealing successfully with Tom's employers and learning to take full responsibility for all household and financial decisions on my own. I even began to feel rather proud of my increasing ability to cope with such matters. Meanwhile Tom's estate was gradually being sorted out, while my own financial position was beginning to look less dire and, eventually, encouraging. I made a conscious decision to view each victory, however minor, as a fresh ray of light in the darkness which had initially threatened to overwhelm me.

As those rays of light increased in number, they began to join up until the resulting expansion of the light began, in its turn, to overwhelm the darkness. And at that point, the horror of the scene I had witnessed began to lose its power to dominate my psyche: I was beginning to work my way free. What I had experienced in my house had been so horrific that to have relinquished my self-discipline at any stage, even briefly, would only have made me feel worse in my private, personal struggle to regain peace of mind. Immersing myself in dealing with the practicalities was, I found, the only way to prevent my being overwhelmed by the sheer enormity of what had happened.

Naturally, though, I couldn't prevent the terrible feeling of longing to send time backwards, to enable us to carry on living as we had once lived, as a couple and as a family. My own life had assumed an impassable emotional divide: life 'before' and life 'after'. I would watch other couples and other families, as they shared a joke or a meal, held hands while walking their dog, or made plans for a celebration – particularly Christmas, of course – and I would swallow down the rising bile of jealousy, and turn away to blink back a certain mistiness in my eyes. But I was not alone in the world by any means. I had always enjoyed an excellent relationship with both my sons, and remained very close to them, but now my adult relationship with each of them developed on a truly profound level, bound as we were even more tightly by the intimacy of love, grief and unparalleled concern through the deepest crisis.

Purely by chance, I discovered that the Chinese word for 'crisis' is composed of two symbols: the first is *Danger* and the second is *Opportunity*. As a family we had certainly survived our own levels of danger, physically and mentally. I could, as the doctor told me, have suffered a fatal heart attack on discovering my husband's body in its hanged state. As could my mother, when two policemen arrived and she thought, however briefly, that I'd been killed on the motorway after driving her home. My sons could have gone off the rails completely, and become alcoholics, drug addicts, or worse. But we had all survived, and found ourselves with new opportunities to reassess and redirect our lives. Mark was moved to the core by the strength of his girlfriend's support, and they are now happily married. Paul grasped the opportunity to re-train and leave the farm to live and work in Europe with Bea, his own, equally supportive girlfriend.

Trips to see each of my sons continue to be refreshing as well as vitally important to all three of us, naturally, enabling us to check on each other's progress while simply enjoying the luxury of being together. I also find myself taking even greater pleasure in glorious scenery, such as the age-old and changeless views in the Lake District, where Mark and his 'Northern family' take me for days spent walking, indulging in the occasional scenic boat trip, visiting favourite cafés and simply drinking in the scenery and the cool, clear air. The therapeutic value of those family excursions is still incalculable.

Back at home, my continuing pleasure in small and seemingly insignificant treats has played its own part in my increasing sense of well-being: everyday pleasures, which were formerly so commonplace as to pass almost unnoticed, are now to be cherished as luxuries. Everything from a bowl of hot, homemade soup on a cold day, to picking fresh flowers from my garden on a warm one.

I'd known this would be the case, because I'd already had first-hand experience, having watched and encouraged a close and dear relative using the same technique to help her deal with this same situation; there had been a previous suicide in my own family. It had happened shortly after Tom and I became engaged, so that Tom himself had already witnessed the after-effects of suicide and seen their devastating consequences on a family, many years before his mind collapsed into its own private version of chaos.

On being demobbed after the Second World War, my uncle had emigrated to America with his wife and their son and daughter. Their son joined the US Navy at the time of the Vietnam War, when he saw action as an officer on board a destroyer. He, in turn, eventually returned to civilian life, apparently happily. In 1980, while my uncle and aunt were in the UK for my grandmother's funeral, my cousin shot himself. His suicide note cited as the cause his feelings of guilt at repeatedly relaying to the ship's gun crew the order to fire, so that he held himself personally responsible for the resulting deaths. He had left an answerphone message (in those days before mobile phones) for his sister just hours before he committed suicide, so she was left to torment herself with the unanswerable question of whether, had she been at home to take that call, she could have saved her brother. The shock accelerated my uncle's cancer, and he died within six months of his son.

Following the deaths of her son and husband, my aunt was left with terrifyingly large financial commitments. My uncle, though normally an astute man, had not taken out mortgage protection insurance. What he had taken out, though, was a second mortgage, to help set up their now dead son in business. And so my aunt, like me thirty-odd years later, had to work through a period of financial difficulty and uncertainty, while also dealing with the aftermath of suicide and, in her case, a natural death in addition to all that. During the following years my aunt and I became increasingly close, with much crossing of the Atlantic and sitting up till the early hours agonising over what could have gone so terribly wrong in the secret recesses of my cousin's mind.

All this meant that I had frequently witnessed the raw and desperate grief of a mother who felt that she should have been able to save her son from himself. But even in my wildest nightmares I could never have imagined that one day, in a then unimaginably terrible future, I would feel the same intensity of pain, but as a wife for her husband. In my immediate family, then, the manner of my cousin's death proved to be a ghastly precursor to my husband's, many years later. Each of these cases of suicide confirmed, with relentless and sickening clarity, the unalterable truth that suicide does indeed set in motion a succession of appalling consequences. However unforeseen and unintentional, those consequences are nonetheless devastatingly painful for the survivors.

By pure coincidence, when my surviving cousin had to phone her parents here in England to break the unspeakable news to them back in 1980, the person who happened to be in the room when my uncle took the call was – my mother. So, when my turn came thirty-two years later, my mother had already had the horrific experience of dealing with both the immediate aftermath of suicide, and the full trauma of its aftershocks. Although even that could not have prepared her for the devastation of the suicide which was yet to come, when she would be required to help pick up the pieces once again, but this time as a mother sharing the agony of her own daughter and her grandsons.

My aunt and I remained close, but knowing of her fragile state of health, it was not my aunt I phoned on that day of endless phone calls after Tom died, but my surviving cousin, who once again had to break the news of a suicide to her mother. And so a strange sense of déjà vu added to my family's sense of unreality. But my aunt's experience had taught me a lot about how to handle the situation and strive to create a feeling of well-being. As my financial position gradually improved, my sense of delight in buying myself a new book, perhaps, or being able to spend a little extra on a family birthday gift, was heightened in intensity by my very recent, salutary reminder that such luxuries should never be taken for granted.

Right from the start, I had felt that I owed it to myself to recover as quickly and completely as I could, although initially, simply staying alive and getting through each day seemed enough to aim for. So it came as something of a surprise when, some months later, I received notification that I was, in fact, dead. As might be expected, my spirits were blithely lifted by the absurdity of this piece of news, although there was evidently a darker undertone. But it's a rather startling feeling when you read your own name on the subject line of a letter, with the word 'deceased' after it. It appears rather final and don't-mind-me, as Winnie-the-Pooh's friend Eeyore might say. And at this point, I should just mention that my middle name is Alice.

The letter in question had been sent originally to my son Mark, who decided it should pass on – in a manner of speaking – to me. This letter stated that a cousin of Pamela Roberts (my late mother-in-law), had died intestate leaving a large sum of money. Initial investigations had revealed that this sum (unspecified) was eligible to be divided among Pamela's children. Her son Tom being deceased, his portion was to be divided between his sons Mark and Paul. All Mark had to do, at this stage, was simply to send authenticated evidence of his identity, plus certified copies of his father's birth and death certificates, to this thoroughly trustworthy, helpful and selfless 'probate research' company. And the name of the late cousin of the late Pamela Roberts?

Alyse Lucy Roberts, deceased.

My instinctive reaction was: how dare anyone tell me I'm dead – I'm certainly not going to take that lying down! Initially I thought I might send a 'stiff' reply, but then I decided not to open that particular can of worms, risking the disclosure of more information. Buried beneath the comic aspect, there was clearly something 'gravely' insidious about this.

My son wasn't about to go dishing out documents, even before the next letter could be expected to arrive, probably requesting an upfront fee to defray the necessary expenses of the 'investigation'. Obviously, any cousin of Pamela Roberts would be rather unlikely to be called Roberts in any case, that being her married name. Presumably the slight changes to my own married name were designed to lend verisimilitude; perhaps to give an impression of continuity within the family, or maybe simply to mislead any cursory investigation. It is possible to obtain details of names which have recently ceased to be in use, for whatever reason, which would include not only my husband's name, but also my married name. This family tree was becoming curiouser and curiouser, as Alyse might say.

However, since I was not dead but very much alive, the feeling was growing that in making a new life for myself, I was going to need a completely fresh start. I knew I couldn't stay at Riverside; the house and its garden had really been unnecessarily large for the two of us, let alone for just the one of me. The household bills were also too large for just the one of me, of course, and it made no sense to maintain a four-bedroomed house purely for those rare occasions when my sons, with their respective partners and eventual families, might visit together. During my first year of living alone, the feeling gradually grew that it would be healthier for me to leave the village and start again elsewhere. I had made friends there, and received many kindnesses since Tom's death, but I was beginning to feel slightly stifled. People obviously felt desperately sorry for me, and had decided that I should be kept busy. I was invited to all manner of clubs, associations and societies – of which the most startling was the Darby and Joan Club for the elderly people of the village (I was 53 years old at the time). Evidently widowhood had aged me by at least twenty years!

I was also viewed as being ripe to take on more 'jobs' in the village, now that I was alone with, apparently, time on my hands. Actually my time was very well filled – given the chance – with my own household, garden and business concerns, plus my ongoing attempts to maintain a regular writing routine. But working at home meant that I was considered available whenever required, and I found my daytime schedule being organised largely for the convenience of other people. With ever-increasing zeal, they felt they were helping me by 'needing' me to perform individual but increasingly time-consuming tasks.

The most insensitive example was the decision by one of the village societies to use my garage to store the many items being collected for a forthcoming jumble sale. But I was told, not asked, about this arrangement. The presence of well-meaning ladies dashing in and out and re-organising my garage, of all places, was the last thing I felt I needed at that point in my recovery, so, for the first time, I politely refused. Such dedicated people are vital to any small community if it is to thrive, naturally, but personally I needed to concentrate on my own recovery and my own attempts to build an independent future. In any case, I was finding that village activities, which had been great fun when there were two of us, could be extremely painful now that I had to smile my way through them alone, while trying not to draw comparisons with those same events attended by Tom and myself during the previous year.

Meanwhile, a new housing estate was about to be built on the outskirts of the village and was causing great excitement. The estate agent's glossy brochure was very enticing, of course, and so I was briefly tempted by the smaller houses there. But I would be going past Riverside every day; walking the dog in that same field behind my former home; going to the same shops and the same viewpoints as I had done with my husband, in those optimistic early days of our new life together in the village. Gradually I came to realise that I simply couldn't do that. I would need to let go completely and start afresh, if I wanted to succeed in my new life as an independent single woman.

And so my wider search began, tentatively at first. Where to go? My main priority was naturally to stay within reach of my mother, although I simply couldn't face a return to that area, or even to the area in between, where I had spent so many years with Tom in our early, carefree days. No: I would need to look elsewhere.

One day towards the end of my first summer alone, I had taken Misty to the South Downs, simply for a change and a picnic: I'd never been there with Tom. Standing there on the cliff top, I gazed at the downland stretching away in one direction and the sea in the other, joined by the line of ancient chalk-white cliffs. All rich in wildlife, history, and a fresh outlook. Wheeling sea birds crying on one side of me, soaring skylarks pouring out their song on the other. I thought of our previous homes, not merely Fleet-ingly, but in particular of the North Cornwall coast where we had been so happy. This Channel coast version was much gentler; less dramatic, perhaps, but certainly less remote, and with a breathtaking vista of its own. Eagerly, I took in the freshness of the sea air and the beauty of the panorama spread out before me.

I had arrived. At a decision, at least.

Chapter 18: A moving experience

On a cold and gloomy January day, I sat alone in my car and looked up at a modest, brand new house on an estate near the edge of the South Downs. It was now just over a year since Tom's death, and the decision I'd taken on that windy clifftop, six months previously, had held firm despite all the rational objections I could think of to oppose it: my friends in the village; the many kindnesses I had been shown there; the prospect of tearing myself up by the roots yet again.

And yet the idea of moving had itself taken root in my mind. But as I looked up at that new house, and glanced again at the floorplan – almost exactly the one I would sketch if asked for my ideal small house – I knew that there was still one rational objection; location. One of a group of new though not identical houses, this ideal home of mine had been built at the edge of a 1970s housing estate, complete with unsightly and unkempt garage blocks, a tired-looking parade of shops, a drab repair garage and a dreary-looking pub. A footpath alongside the house led to the main road into the town itself. I sighed and folded away the floorplan.

But that little house had lodged itself in my mind, and refused to move out. So, a few weeks later, I drove down and stared at it again; just to convince myself that it really was too hemmed-in and suburban. After all, I'd already moved away from suburbia and become used to a village; could I really swap its locally-stocked community shop for a standard mini-supermarket? Well yes, actually, I was beginning to think perhaps I could!

And so I arranged a viewing. The house itself was all I'd anticipated, though the rear garden seemed tiny, of course. But if I wanted a small, modern house, it was bound to be on a small plot. And I knew I mustn't compare it with Riverside's garden, as I couldn't have it both ways: wanting a small garden because I'm really no gardener, and then complaining because the garden is small! But from the moment I stepped into its hallway, that house had the right 'feel' as my potential new home. Plus, suburban street lights and pavements did have an appeal, especially for a lone dog-walker on dark evenings.

The situation of the house had all the features which I knew Tom would most despise: a shared driveway with another new house, on one side; the public footpath on the other side; back-to-back with the other new houses; wedged at the top of a long and tightly-packed close with public parking beyond the footpath. But Tom wasn't here to despise it. After viewing the house again, this time with my mother, and discussing it with my sons, I made an offer, which was accepted.

Moving house is generally acknowledged to be one of life's most stressful experiences, being second only to divorce, although perhaps I personally have another contender for that rather dubious distinction. But the part that really scared me wasn't the idea of moving to a new area, because I'd already proved I could do that; no, it was the actual logistics, and the idea of doing it all completely alone.

Having made my decision, I couldn't help but think ahead to the entire process; knowing how much there would be to do, I had to fight down a rising sense of panic. So I simply made myself concentrate solely on each next task, and tried not to look too far ahead.

Initially the sale of Riverside looked set to go swimmingly, appropriately enough, with an unsolicited direct approach from a local man. I advised him that the house would be sold through my estate agent, to whom he was welcome to make an offer. Unfortunately, this potential buyer was not in quite the position to proceed as he had led me to believe. Consequently, when my house was actually sold elsewhere, this gentleman – who was fully aware of my circumstances – phoned me and proceeded to hurl abuse. Apparently he felt that being first to view the house gave him some sort of pre-existing right to buy it in his own good time and on his own terms. After shouting assorted insults at me, he was forced to pause simply to draw breath, so I took the opportunity to inform him that his behaviour would be referred to my solicitor. He slammed the phone down. Although this man was only a minor bully, the episode unsettled me, making me wonder whether I had recovered sufficient strength to enable me to deal with such people. One prominent villager had described this man as:

"A decent chap and the favoured candidate to buy Riverside", leading me to wonder who was actually selling this house, myself or a committee of village elders!

The conveyancing process continued on its stately course, with the usual hiccups and interruptions, and meanwhile I continued to sell, donate and recycle a seemingly endless stream of furniture and possessions. The therapeutic value of doing so remained just as strong as it had done in the early months after Tom's death. Having made paper templates of my remaining furniture, I arranged to visit my new house again, and was overjoyed to find that the templates seemed to fit perfectly! So now I began to get excited about my fresh start.

I'd been feeling that a straightforward house number wasn't quite sufficient, somehow: I'd been so proud of the name Riverside, which had seemed to give our house character. Tom and I had felt the need to change its name from the original 'The Doghouse', since it seemed unfair for the house to be named for Misty but not Jerry. We could have changed it to The Dog and Tortoise, of course, but that would have sounded like a pub, and I didn't relish the prospect of strangers turning up on the doorstep demanding a pint of beer and a bag of crisps. So The Doghouse had become Riverside.

Although the allocated house number would do the job this time, I felt my new house deserved something more. But I was concerned that giving it a name might appear pretentious; then I realised that it was to be my very own house, I would be answerable to no one except myself, and I could do exactly as I pleased! Obviously I didn't want to re-use Riverside, and anyway it wasn't appropriate, as I would have another house behind me instead of a river. But from my study upstairs, I'd be able to look out at the ridge of the Downs, dotted with sheep and surmounted by skylarks.

The skylark has always been my favourite bird. Not only for its exquisitely beautiful song, but also for the character which its behaviour seems to bring to that insignificant-looking little songster: it always aims high; it has enormous capacity; it is undaunted. All qualities I find 'highly' admirable!

The main point about Skylarks was that, although substantially smaller, it was to be no second-best after Riverside; right from the start, I viewed it as simply a far more suitable house for the next chapter of my life. The mere fact of its being brand new, and so much smaller, would be a great relief after the upkeep of Riverside. Skylarks was to prove ideal as a home for me, giving me the freedom I needed to recover myself. It fulfilled my expectations of being a light and bright house, exuding a sense of freshness and optimism. I knew there would be teething troubles with the house itself, naturally, though these could all be overcome. Gradually, too, I would get to know my neighbours and establish my new routines, both for household matters and in my newly re-established working life.

And so I had come full circle, and what an unimaginably, devastatingly moving experience it had all been. Within three years, the family home where we'd brought up our children had been sold, as had our beloved holiday home in Cornwall. We had moved to a traditional village to begin a new life in preparation for Tom's retirement. That cosy prospect had been destroyed, along with our marriage itself, in the most hideous and cruel circumstances as our retirement dream turned into a nightmare. Consequently, I had endured an ordeal which had plunged me into the deepest and most searing pain, from which I was now emerging into complete independence, for the first time in my life. But to enable me to go on meaningfully with my own life, I would need to find a different sort of strength; the courage to let Tom go, finally, along with the remains of my anger and guilt.

If the coroner was correct in his assertions, firstly that Tom was of sound mind when he hanged himself, and secondly that I was lying about the undated letter, so that the row to which it referred took place not three years earlier but shortly before he committed suicide, then it must follow that I was indeed guilty of being a contributory cause of my husband's death. Conversely, since I was right over the letter, and if the doctor was right in his unequivocal assertion that Tom was *not* of sound mind, then his death was caused by that most insidious of potentially fatal illnesses – depression.

No one can answer the question of which version is correct, in the absence of Tom himself. Which means that I have indeed come full circle, ending by returning to the question with which I started: *May I speak to the deceased, please?* And the answer to that question remains, of course, a resounding *No*. But to achieve my own lasting peace, and make sense of both Tom's death and my continuing life, I must steer a sensible course between those two opposing professional views, the legal versus the medical, to allow myself both intellectual and emotional release.

As a layman – and more importantly as Tom's life partner – my own view is that there must have been some developing mental problem which caused him to become suicidal, as thoughts of suicide are not a normal reaction to stress or unhappiness. Whatever the form or extent of that mental instability may have been, his refusal to recognise that something was wrong, in the initial stages, was entirely within his normal character.

The consequent refusal to admit to needing help was part of Tom's unbreakable code of self-reliance, which was in itself a lifelong characteristic. He could have confided in our family doctor, or his boss, a welfare officer within the company, his cousin; his wife. But he chose not to. He forced himself to battle on alone, even as his thoughts and feelings darkened to develop, unchecked, into something far more dangerous and ultimately unstoppable. The anger which I bore against Tom for so long, stemmed less from the fact of his suicide itself than from his underlying failure to acknowledge that he could no longer cope alone with his inner turmoil. Had he acknowledged the need for help, for some form of human contact, perhaps his problems could have been dealt with before he reached the point of no return. But since Tom cannot now answer for himself, I cannot possibly know when or how that point of no return occurred, or what had already gone on inside his closed and secretive mind. And once I had learned to accept that inescapable truth, my anger against Tom became pointless: it arose from an unanswerable question posed to a dead man, and so if I let that anger fester, it would cause further harm to no one except myself.

My conclusion, then, had to be that we must each take responsibility for our own actions. And if I require Tom to bear responsibility for his suicide, then it follows that I must bear responsibility for my own recovery from the effects of his suicide on me. That conclusion has proved pivotal, not only in my struggle to regain control of my life, but also in my intensely private struggle to remember the real Tom, and to lay my anger against him to rest. My attempts to see beyond Tom dead, so horrifically and vindictively, to Tom alive, warm and caring, were for so long obscured by anger and pain that the real Tom had almost passed from my consciousness. That in itself would have been a tragic distortion of our married life, and I had already borne enough tragedy and enough distortion of the truth. And so I set about learning to regard my marriage, despite its unnatural ending, as complete.

After Tom died, various well-meaning people liked to tell me:

"You'll be bound to meet someone else", satisfied in the belief that they were offering me comfort and hope.

Whether or not that will ever happen remains to be seen, but I am open-minded about my future, and determined to avoid any hint of bitterness creeping into my character because of the past. For now, though, my comforts are simply knowing that I have survived, and seeing my sons' happiness with their respective partners, while remembering all that Tom and I shared during so many genuinely happy years of our own. That way, I find myself able to live fully in the present, without nurturing either any hope or any dread of my own possible situation in the future.

As I stand at the edge of the South Downs with my faithful dog Misty, and gaze beyond that timeless landscape to the sea, my spirits are lifted and my mind is calmed. So much has been lost to me, but by no means everything.

I have my sons, each of them many hundreds of miles away but emotionally just as close to me as they ever were; even more so, after our shared experience. I have my mother, in her nineties now, increasingly frail but still more concerned for her family than for herself, and as shining an example of strength and resolution as she ever was. I have my friends, each only a phone call or an email away, providing me with the bedrock of stability that comes from a fund of shared experience. I have a degree of financial security unimaginable in the immediate aftermath of Tom's death. I have my own home, far better suited to my needs than Riverside could ever have been, where I have been able to recover my equanimity in the way that only nature could dictate. The horror of Tom's death will continue its natural and proper process of receding, gradually eclipsed by the consciousness that I have my own evolving place in this living, changing world, and that my life retains its sense of order and purpose.

After all, my own story is not yet finished! But to enable me to turn to the next chapter of my life, I must first close this previous one; finally, honestly and peacefully. What do I take with me, then, into my own, individual next chapter? I am no longer quite the same person I used to be; obviously, such a traumatic experience must leave its own indelible mark, but I should like to think that my outlook has been broadened, in line with all I have experienced. Certainly my sensitivities are heightened: notably, I hope, towards other people's pain, along with a realisation that pain can be carefully concealed, even if not quite as thoroughly as Tom's pain was concealed. I am more acutely aware of the fragility of life itself. That in turn has brought me increased awareness of the beauty of the natural world, the joy of family relationships, the importance of friendship, and the inestimable value of pure human kindness, willingly offered and gladly accepted.

My marriage to Tom is over, but its true and lasting legacy remains our sons, and that unalterable truth brings me immeasurable comfort. I am incredibly proud of the way in which Mark and Paul have borne their tragedy, as I know the 'real' Tom would have been. Our sons are both leading happy, fulfilled and balanced lives.

The expanse of time since my husband's death has been no emotional wasteland, but has been filled with the most extraordinarily moving experiences of my life. One of the many truths I have learned is that no event, however terrible in itself, is totally without the possibility of producing good consequences, and therefore of providing at least a part of its own redemption.

With the unstinting support of my family and friends, I have emerged from my ordeal with my own sanity intact. I have run the full gamut of emotions myself, while witnessing an enormous range of behaviour in others, from demonstrations of real love and deeply moving kindness, to official indifference and obstruction, along with a very few incidences of personal antagonism and unkindness. But the good all around me has without any doubt outweighed and even obliterated the bad, and continues to do so.

And that, in itself, is truly an uplifting and heartening conclusion to be able to draw, from such an experience as this chapter of my life has been.

13927545R00073

Printed in Great Britain
by Amazon.co.uk, Ltd.,
Marston Gate.